FINDING YOUR *Voice*

A GUIDE TO COLLEGE COMPOSITION

JAMES P. AUSTIN | ELIZABETH BREWER

Central Connecticut State University

Kendall Hunt
publishing company

Cover image © Shutterstock.com

Kendall Hunt
publishing company

www.kendallhunt.com
Send all inquiries to:
4050 Westmark Drive
Dubuque, IA 52004-1840

CONTENTS

STUDENT ESSAYS

Finding Your Voice: A Guide to College Composition

by Elizabeth Brewer

The book you're reading is a guide for your first-year writing classes at CCSU: WRT 100, 105, and 110. And unlike many other textbooks, this one was written *by* professors at CCSU especially with *you* in mind. The chapters focus on the writing assignments we know you'll work on in your writing classes, and we thought about concepts and terminology you'll need. We gathered up the tips, exercises, and examples we use and wrote them down in a book tailored for the class you're in now. How cool is that?

We titled this book, *Finding Your Voice: A Guide to College Composition*, because we're doing just that in first-year writing classes. Of course, you already have a voice (literally and figuratively). You take stands, you tell stories, you make others laugh. You have a unique perspective. In those ways, you have already found your voice. But as you write new types of essays and try out new processes, you'll develop that voice further. Sometimes, we compare finding our voice to choosing an outfit for a new situation. Let's imagine you start a new job in an office. When you choose an outfit for the first day of work, you'll consider the basics you know about what people wear to office environments, but you won't be trying to look like a general employee. You'll be trying to blend your knowledge of workwear with your own style and with what clothing you already have. Figuring out the kinds of things *you* wear to work is an act of discovery. Finding your voice as a writer is similar. You might not know, for example, what you sound like as an academic writer. Your job this semester is to learn what college-level writing sounds like in general, but also what *your specific* college-level writing is like. And that is a discovery process that involves trying out new methods, getting lots of feedback, and revising. This book and your professor are guides through that process.

Introduction to Rhetoric

This semester, you're writing as a process and familiarizing yourself with expectations for academic writing. You're learning *a lot*. It can help to simplify all these things under one central concept, and we can do that for you. Here it is: At the core, we're learning about rhetoric, which we define as the study of communication. When we study rhetoric, we are building a toolkit of ways we can read texts and understand them in their context. We are learning to talk about how writers effectively (or not so effectively) try to persuade their readers to agree with them. We are learning to say, "I know what that writer is doing there! And here's why it works." Learning to read rhetorically empowers you to understand messages you encounter and decide for yourself if you agree with them or like them—because you'll have a toolkit to decipher their meaning and the strategies the writer used. You will also use rhetoric yourself. As a writer, you are not only studying rhetoric, but you are using the strategies you learn about.

Because rhetoric is the central concept we're learning this semester—and it is discussed in every chapter—we want to start building your toolkit of concepts right here in this Introduction.

Rhetorical Situations

Your instructor might introduce you to something called the rhetorical situation, which is the context surrounding a text you're reading. When you try to identify what the rhetorical situation is for an essay, you are trying to articulate a number of things about it. First, you want to state the author's purpose. In other words, you'll articulate their reason for writing and what they are hoping to accomplish. Second, you'll identify the intended audience that the writer seems to be targeting. Note that the audience for a text is not whoever happens to read it. The audience is the group of people the writer wants to persuade. It is the group that the writer has in mind and is writing to. Third, you'll identify any events that happened in the world or in the writer's life that can help you understand their position. The context can provide valuable information about why a writer is arguing something at that time. Finally, you'll want to consider the genre you're reading. For example, is it a newspaper article, a scholarly book chapter, or a tweet? These are all different genres, and audiences expect specific conventions to be followed for each of them. Genres themselves put limits on what (or how much) a writer can include, and they offer unique affordances, or things a writer can do. For example, in an online newspaper article the writer has a word limit, but also has the ability to link to their sources and embed images and videos. These are limitations and benefits of the genre.

When you read something new and are trying to understand it, a helpful tool is asking yourself, "What is the writer's rhetorical situation?" And that is true even if the writer is *you*. You can articulate your own rhetorical situation, and use it to check that your draft really helps persuade your particular audience.

Rhetorical Appeals

The other part of the rhetorical tool kit you'll build in first-year writing is an understanding of rhetorical appeals. Rhetorical appeals are methods a writer uses to persuade their audience. The most common rhetorical appeals are defined below (and we talk about them again in the Genres chapter.) Simply put, rhetorical appeals are strategies a writer tries, and sometimes these strategies work better than other times. Your job as a thoughtful reader is to identify the appeals, hypothesize why the writer employed them, and ultimately determine how effective a writer has been at using their methods. Let's take a look at the most common appeals:

Ethos—appeal to credibility. Appeals to ethos include all the ways a writer establishes trust with the reader. This might include listing the writer's credentials, using sources effectively, or speaking from experience.

Pathos—appeal to emotion. Appeals to pathos include all the ways a writer moves the reader to feel something. Those feelings can be anything from joy, anger, silliness, or even empathy or engagement with the writer. An appeal to emotion could be a joke or a heart-wrenching story. Or it could simply be the way a writer uses "we" to talk about an experience that they think the audiences shares; this might produce an emotional bond and sense of community—just from a pronoun choice.

Logos—appeal to logic. Appeals to logos include all the ways a writer signals their argument is reasonable and makes sense. These signals can include clear organization, well-developed paragraphs, concise sentences, and many other aspects of an essay.

Kairos—appeal to timeliness. Appeals to kairos refer to arguments that take context into consideration effectively. A writer who is considering ways of appealing to kairos will ask themselves what the audience currently knows and cares about, and the writer will try to tap into those current conditions to better make a point. A good example of appealing to kairos would be if a company that sells generators ran ads right after a storm that knocked out power for many people. Because that experience of losing power is fresh in people's minds, they might be especially interested in buying generators to prepare for future storms.

When you identify rhetorical appeals, remember that you are looking for attempts the writer is making to persuade the audience. Appeals are not features of an essay that are simply *there*, and finding them is not like finding "Easter eggs" that have been hiding in an essay. You are not looking for logic, or emotion, or trustworthiness in an essay because we can't actually find these things in an essay. *What we can find are choices a writer has made* that are likely to move a reader to feel something (that'd be an appeal to pathos) or are likely to make a reader think an argument makes good sense (that'd be an appeal to logos). When an author cites sources transparently, this could be an appeal to ethos because a reader is likely to conclude that the writer is trustworthy because the sources are clear. It can be tricky at first to understand that rhetorical appeals are strategies and not qualities of a text, but with practice, it will become easier.

Chapter Overview

As you navigate this book, you'll find the following chapters:

Chapter 1: Genres in Writing—This chapter provides an overview of the types of papers you'll be writing in WRT 105 and WRT 110. For each type of paper described in this chapter, we show you a sample outline and give you examples and exercises. Our goal for this chapter is to help you understand the expectations of particular types of essays and writing assignments.

Chapter 2: Getting Started—Here we share strategies for the early stages of the writing process, when you are forming ideas and going from a blank page to an outline or you're coming up with research questions. This chapter gives you a place to begin.

Chapter 3: Writing Processes—This chapter deals with the many things associated with the writing process once you have started. It takes you through drafting to revising, editing, and proofreading. And, importantly, it also discusses the benefit of peer review and receiving feedback from others. No matter what genre you're writing in, the information in this chapter will apply.

Chapter 4: Writing Craft—This chapter focuses on developing your voice and writing style. It gets specific about strategies you can use on the sentence level to affect how readers understand your voice and position on an issue.

Chapter 5: Engaging with Sources—You might think about this chapter as the one about research. It provides guidance on finding, using, and citing sources. But it also discusses strategies for writing summaries, building annotated bibliographies, and analyzing sources.

Chapter 6: The 105P Workshop—This chapter is specifically for students in WRT 105 because it explains how the 105P Workshop functions. We provide answers to our frequently asked questions about the workshop, and we give you ideas for making the most of this unique, supportive writing environment.

Conclusion: Exit Interview: Now That You Have Completed First-Year Writing, What Comes Next?—The concluding chapter encourages you to think beyond your first-year writing course. It helps you consider ways you can take what you have learned about writing and apply it to other classes and professional contexts.

Your instructor may assign you chapters in the order they appear in this book, or you may be asked to read chapters out of order or leave some out. That is fine! Even if you aren't assigned every chapter in the book, we encourage you to use it as a resource that works for you. Everything here was written with you in mind.

We can't wait to work with you as you find your voice in first-year writing at CCSU!

CHAPTER 1

Genres in Writing

by Rebecca Arruda

Introduction

Think of the last movie you saw. Was it a horror movie or romance? Was it an action film or comedy? Each one of these categories is known as a genre, which the *Oxford English Dictionary* defines as "A particular style or category of works of art; esp. a type of literary work characterized by a particular form, style, or purpose" (oed.com).

There are many genres of movies and each time you choose to view one, you have certain expectations as an audience member. For example, you would expect a comedy to have jokes, a lighthearted or silly plotline, and probably upbeat music. In contrast, your expectations of a horror movie would probably include a scary soundtrack to elicit tension, screams to evoke fear, and probably some good, old-fashioned blood! If a majority of these expectations are not met, you will likely be disappointed with the film. Failing the audience's expectations is the last thing a movie producer wants on their resume, and thankfully, successful movie makers know how to adhere to the correct genre. Interestingly, the same categorizing that happens with movies also occurs in writing.

In addition to considering genre, just like a filmmaker, an author has various other factors to consider, such as setting out writing with a purpose, always keeping their audience and chosen genre in the forefront of their mind. The definition of purpose is simple. It's the reason an author writes a text. These reasons can vary, and also overlap. Some examples of purpose are to entertain, to inform, and to persuade. Very rarely will you come across a piece of writing that wasn't created for a reason, because, let's be honest, what would be the point of writing something that wasn't going to accomplish any kind of goal?

As a reader, you have certain expectations, depending on which genre you are reading. If you are reading a news story from a mainstream source, you expect to be informed, but if you read an op-ed column, you expect to read the writer's opinion, and understand they are most likely trying to persuade you. If you peruse a satirical website, you anticipate being entertained, knowing the text is laced with humor and sarcasm. Being aware of the genre is important as a reader, but it's equally important to keep in mind when you are the writer. When you are asked to compose an essay in your writing class, or any class, remember to consider who your intended audience might be (there could be more than one group) and be sure to meet their expectations in whatever genre you are writing about. For example, if you are asked to write a narrative essay, a story about your own life and experiences, you would *not* want to write a research paper using outside sources. In this type of writing, *you* are the expert, and the audience wants to hear your story directly from you.

In this chapter, we will examine a number of different genres of writing and explore the deeper meaning of each: personal writing/narrative, rhetorical analysis, argumentation, and reflection/metacognition. You may be assigned several of these genres, and this chapter will guide you in understanding what each one entails and get you thinking about how best to approach them. We will also discuss writing in different genres for rhetorical effect, which is how a writer elicits a response in a reader, often looking to persuade them. Let's begin by considering the concept of genre as a whole.

Exercise

Choose a movie genre (romance, action, horror etc.) and list the expectations you would have, going in to see this type of movie. **Brainstorm** as many expectations as you can below.

_____   _____   _____

_____   _____   _____

_____   _____   _____

Now, imagine if several of these expectations were missing from the movie? How would it leave you feeling? Probably disappointed and unsatisfied. Just as in movies, we want to meet the audience's expectations in writing. The goal is to leave the reader satisfied that the genre's expectations were met.

Although a writer should approach a text having a genre in mind, it is okay to get creative and combine genres in order to reach a larger audience or just to have some fun, pushing the traditional conventional limits of them. For example, many modern television shows combine genres, allowing their audiences a wide array of emotions. If you merge a drama with a comedy, we get the new genre of "dramedy." If we blend a romance with a comedy, it is a "romcom." Once you are comfortable writing in a particular genre, you might experiment with combining genres or disrupting readers' expectations. But you'll want to make sure any deviation from genre expectations is intentional on your part and that your instructor supports this.

Now let's dig into some common genres you might be assigned in your composition class.

Personal Writing/Narrative

When you think of writing a narrative, you might flash back to middle school and the famous "tell me what you did over the summer" assignment. While this writing task has a useful purpose, as a college student you will be asked to write beyond a simple restating of events. In an academic setting, narratives serve to not only tell your story, but to help your readers experience something *with* you. By using sensory images, vivid descriptions, and specific details, you can capture your audience's attention and provide them with a story that is engaging and has a larger message. A personal narrative benefits both the writer and the reader in several ways. As a writer, it allows you to gain more self-awareness and knowledge of your past, it aids you in understanding your experiences, and may even help you to establish future goals. A benefit to the reader is that they can learn something by understanding and reflecting on another person's experience.

Reading a text, such as a narrative essay, allows us to get inside the author's head in a way no other mode of communication can. If written with enough sensory images, vivid descriptions, and specific details, a reader can feel like they are joining the writer on a personal journey. We can feel their emotions, see their surroundings, and even hear the sounds they are describing.

Narratives can also be written to present and prove an argument. For example, think about your journey to college. There are probably dozens, if not hundreds of decisions and events that lead you to the place you are now. From your grades and interests in school, to extracurricular involvements, and perhaps your parent's and teachers' influence, all these things coming together guided you in choosing whether to pursue college and where to attend. If you wrote a narrative about your journey to college, it might illuminate your reasons for attending college. It could also allow your professor and fellow students to get to know you better, or it could establish, or re-establish, your future goals.

The following is the opening paragraph of Aaliyah Brown's essay titled "Go Blue Devils, I Guess." Here you can see how she engages with the audience by using sensory images and specific details to relay her personal narrative, all the while keeping true to the narrative genre format.

"Well go Blue Devils, I guess," is what my Aunty Kesha said to me after I informed her of my decision to attend Central Connecticut State University (CCSU). She followed the statement with a breathy chuckle. Her sarcasm was fairly unwarranted in the situation, especially after all the discussions that we had about where I should go to college. I think it is a complete understatement to say that it was not my plan to attend CCSU. Ever since I was born, the plan has always been for me to go to college. Now that it was senior year, the ball was rolling. I was accepted into all but one of the schools I applied to, even my dream school. All I had to do was make a decision. Suddenly, disaster strikes. My father has a stroke. He is put in the Intensive Care Unit because he cannot breathe on his own. We do not know why this happened or when he will be better again. My family and finances are in crisis. So is my future. The plan changes and so does my entire outlook on life. All of a sudden, in just a short amount of time, CCSU became the most ideal place for me to go. I chose to attend Central because, for some reason that I am not aware of yet, I am supposed to be here. If my father had never gotten sick, I would have had the capability to attend college out of state and go wherever I wanted; however, I believe that I was put in this situation at a specific time when it was meant for me to make a decision so that I would stay in Connecticut. So that I would attend CCSU (Brown[1]).

Exercise

Brainstorm by **freewriting** (write a few sentences continuously, without stopping) and answer the following questions about your decision to go to college. Use these answers to kickstart a personal narrative essay of your own.

- Why are you in college?
- What do you hope to learn, practice, and do here?
- Upon graduation, what do you expect to be able to know, do, and accomplish?

Using Dialogue to Tell Your Story

In most genres, dialogue is unnecessary. You will use direct quotes in your researched argument and rhetorical analysis essays (read further for more information on these). But in narrative writing, it is often useful to use dialogue to help *show* your story to the reader, rather than just *tell* them about it. Below is an example of how using dialogue (conversation) in your narrative brings the story to life and helps the reader feel they are experiencing events with you. Here is an excerpt from CCSU student Ryan Zambrzycki's essay titled "A Programmed Response."

---

[1] © Aaliyah Brown

A week before this, I was at my house just relaxing on the weekend, brainlessly watching YouTube videos in our dim but nicely furnished basement. I walked up the pine stairs my dad made himself (just like everything else down there), and saw my dad in the kitchen just staring at me. Little to my surprise, my mom was talking to him a minute before I got upstairs about my college decision. She just happened to leave and went out on a walk right as I got there.

"Raijan (Polish way of saying my name, but not a Polish name), your mom told me you didn't want to go to college. You know, I don't know if I even have worked most of the time. You could make so much more money going to school to be a physical therapist or doctor." He spoke with his usual broken English, with a heavy Polish accent.

"Ok, but I want to help you. I don't really see any benefit from going to university," I told him.

"But you're smart. Smart people go to college!" He bluntly replied[2].

You can see by this short excerpt that the dialogue pulls the reader into the narrative and makes you want to read more!

Exercise

To practice writing dialogue of your own, think about a conversation you had with someone in the last week. In 1 or 2 pages, jot down the conversation to the best of your memory. Indent each time a new person speaks and use quotation marks to make it clear that you are indicating the spoken word.

Sometimes, seeing a sample outline can help us understand a genre. While you don't need to follow this model exactly when you write a narrative, you can study it to learn more about how the genre works.

Narrative Outline Template

Your Road to College

I. Intro paragraph
   A. Hook (an opening sentence or two to get your reader's attention - may write this last)
   B. Background sentences (why are you about to tell this story?)
   C. Thesis (argument) (I chose to come to Central because......)

II. Body paragraphs
   A. Address your thesis - each paragraph should address your reasons individually and make a claim.
   B. Give evidence to support your claim (a conversation or example)
   C. Explain how your evidence proves your claim.

III. Conclusion (restate your thesis and leave the audience with a take-away)

Rhetorical Analysis

When most people hear the word **rhetoric**, they think it has something to do with politics, or they may be thinking of a **rhetorical question**, which is a question asked in order to create a dramatic effect or to make a point rather than to get an answer (oed.com). People who use rhetoric

---

[2] © Ryan Zambrzycki

effectively can be masterful artists at getting their point across and convincing others to agree with them. This is why many call rhetoric an art form. Rhetoric is also used in writing, and this section will address the ways a writer can purposefully use it to persuade their audience. First, let's define what rhetoric is: it's the art of effective or persuasive writing. It uses various methods to convince, influence, and please a reader. This means a writer is looking to persuade their audience to their point of view.

There are numerous techniques available to a writer, and they choose which ones will best move their audience to change their thinking or take action. The techniques we will be examining closely are the appeals to:

- ethos
- pathos
- logos
- kairos

A rhetorical analysis essay is something most college students will be asked to write at some point in their university career and your WRT 105/110 professor will very likely assign you one during the semester. It's a useful genre because it teaches us how to read with focus and intention and how to analyze the choices another writer has made. By examining rhetorical techniques, and considering both how and why a writer employs them, we can learn the art of using these techniques ourselves to help persuade our own audiences. Let's start by defining the rhetorical techniques listed above.

Ethos—appeal to credibility. Appeals to ethos include all the ways a writer establishes trust with the reader.

Pathos—appeal to emotion. Appeals to pathos include all the ways a writer moves the reader to feel something. Those feelings can be anything from joy, anger, silliness, or even empathy or engagement with the writer.

Logos—appeal to logic. Appeals to logos include all the ways a writer signals their argument is reasonable and makes sense. These signals can include clear organization, well developed paragraphs, concise sentences, and many other aspects of an essay.

Kairos—appeal to timeliness. Appeals to kairos refer to arguments that take context into consideration effectively. A writer who is considering ways of appealing to kairos will ask themselves what the audience currently knows and cares about, and the writer will try to tap into those current conditions to better make a point.

When you are asked to write a rhetorical analysis essay, your WRT 105/110 professor is looking for you to analyze and evaluate another writer's work. (Sometimes it will be a speech, film, ad, or something else.) You will examine how the author uses the four appeals and how well they use them to persuade the audience to think a certain way.

Let's look at an example from CCSU student Maslin Laberge. Here, in Laberge's essay titled "Rhetorical Analysis of Kenneth Goldsmith," he is analyzing Goldsmith's use of logos to persuade his audience. Laberge notes in his essay that Goldsmith "provides a common objection to being online and gives rationale as to why the reader should doubt it. However, …Goldsmith uses anecdotal evidence for his arguments, rather than rigorous logic and scientific studies" (Laberge 13[3]).

---

[3] © Maslin Laberge

Maslin is not only showing where Goldsmith uses logos, he is analyzing why he is using it, along with how well he is using it.

Study this outline to deepen your understanding of rhetorical analysis as a genre. If you are assigned a rhetorical analysis essay, you might use this outline as a guide, or you might make other decisions about organization and structure. However you use the outline, you can read it and draw conclusions about what rhetorical analysis essays look like and you can note any questions you have for your instructor.

Rhetorical Analysis Outline Template

I. Intro paragraph
   A. Hook (something to draw the reader in, may be written last)
   B. Summary of article/background info
   C. Thesis (How well (or not) the rhetorical choices the author makes work together to convey the purpose of the article to the intended audience)

II. Context paragraph
   A. Author, place of publication, date
   B. What is the general knowledge of the intended audience about the subject at the time?

III. – VII. Body Paragraphs (intertwine your analysis of different rhetorical devices/give suggestions on how the author could improve to better connect with the audience). All paragraph topic sentences (first sentence of the paragraph) should be a claim of your own and refer back to the thesis - do not begin with a quote or question.
   A. Tone and Word Choice
   B. Ethos and Pathos
   C. Kairos and the Timeliness of the Writer's Argument

VIII. Conclusion
   A. Restate thesis
   B. Again discuss how well (or not) the rhetorical choices work together as a whole to convey the purpose of the article to the audience.
   C. Give your reader something to think about (end with a statement, famous quote, or rhetorical question).

Argumentation

Of all the writing genres you are likely to engage in WRT 100, 105, and 110, you may feel most familiar with the argument essay. When you write an argument, you seek to persuade your audience to change their way of thinking, take some sort of action, feel motivated to find out more about an issue, or encourage informed debate. Argumentation often requires you to find outside sources, but you are extending what others have written by adding your own perspective through your essay. Think of it as joining an existing conversation in which you have a particular stance or claim on the topic being discussed.

Most WRT 105/110 classes will ask you to write a researched argument essay. Through your research process, which will gather outside sources, you will state your claim in response to these other sources (which are really just arguments made by others). These outside sources might vary and come in the form of academic articles, popular articles, books, interviews, and videos. Your professor will let you know the kinds of sources that they expect you to use and a librarian can help you determine if they are credible. Your writing will not be just a summarization of what others have claimed, but you will be adding your unique voice to the existing debate to further your own argument. See the chapter "Engaging with Sources" for further information.

The knowledge you develop about rhetoric and the rhetorical appeals will be incredibly useful as you draft an argument essay. *You* are in control of which rhetorical elements will work best to persuade your audience. By using credible sources, you will establish ethos in your essay. By using pathos, you can elicit an emotional response and establish a closer connection with your audience. In using logos, you can logically guide your reader into thinking about the subject in a new way. Finally, by using kairos, you can plan ways to explain your point that will matter to readers *now*, in a context they care about.

Let's look at an excerpt of a researched argument essay, paying attention to how the author synthesizes sources with their own argument. CCSU student Marc Perras writes in his essay "The United States Was Wrong to Withdraw from Afghanistan." The first reason as to why the United States should have not withdrawn its military from Afghanistan is to protect the people of Afghanistan from the Taliban's unethical rule. In "Afghanistan War Was the United States Right to Have Withdrawn from Afghanistan?" it states: "The Taliban resurgence was particularly strong in Helmand, a southern province where corruption and abuse of power among administrators appointed by Karzai had fueled popular discontent. In Helmand and other provinces, the Taliban infiltrated villages, secured the loyalty of local elders, and assassinated officials or villagers with suspected allegiances to the Afghan state or ISAF" (1[4]). This shows the basic civil liberties that are being broken every day under Taliban rule. The people are led with an iron fist and any that speak out are killed on the spot. This is no way for humans to live and should not be allowed to occur. A withdrawal only exemplifies these examples and every day since America left, we continue to have blood on our hands.

From reading this passage you can see the researched argument genre is about using your own arguments, blended with outside sources to give you the most persuasive and highest impact message possible.

Outline Template for Argument Research Essay

I. **Introduction**
    A. Hook
    B. Background information
    C. Thesis statement

II. **Counterargument Paragraph (can be placed before your body paragraphs, after them, or the opposing views can be integrated into your body paragraphs and responded to there)**
    A. Identify the opposing side of view - what are their arguments?
    B. Validate the other side - how are they being logical?
    C. Briefly refute the opposing point of view - here's why your viewpoints are more valid

III. **Body Paragraphs (as many as you need)**
    A. Claim
    B. Evidence/Source
    C. Explanation

IV. **Conclusion**
    A. Reword thesis
    B. Give the audience something to take away/think about. Consider using a rhetorical question or a famous quote.

---

[4] © Marc Perras

Reflective Writing/Metacognition

The genre of reflective writing is a task that you might view as "extra," but it serves a valuable purpose and is an essential part of the writing process and an important genre. After your paper is complete it is helpful to reflect on what went well during the writing process, what didn't, and steps that can be taken to improve in your future essays. First, let's define what reflective writing is. Reflective writing is a process of identifying, questioning, and assessing knowledge, the way we perceive events, feelings, and actions. And metacognition is awareness or analysis of one's own learning or thinking processes (merriam-webster.com). (See the chapter on the 105P Workshop and the Conclusion for more discussion about reflecting on what we have learned.) When we write about something we created, our process, or what we learned in a class, we get a better sense of the knowledge we have gained so we can apply it to future situations. It can make our hard work feel worth it and give us a well-deserved sense of satisfaction.

Writing a reflective essay is beneficial to both students and professors alike, and should be used as part of the complete writing process. It helps you by providing a framework to think differently about responding to a learning experience, and it gives an opportunity to gain self-knowledge. It helps your teachers make purposeful changes to improve students' outcomes. Letting your professor know where you struggled and where you excelled can aid them in identifying patterns in their classes' writing as a whole. They may choose to approach teaching methods differently in their future classes. This means by giving feedback and analyzing your own writing, you are also helping subsequent students get an even better learning experience!

Reflective writing is also a way to evaluate how you will take the knowledge you learn in your WRT 100, WRT 105, or WRT 110 class and transfer it to your future classes. Composition classes are required for all majors for the purpose of giving you the basic foundations in writing. Once you learn these foundations of essay writing, you can use these skills in any subject.

Exercise

To get you started on writing reflectively, answer the following questions about your own writing.

1. How do you perceive yourself as a writer?
2. What do you like/dislike about your writing?
3. What are your strengths/weaknesses in writing?
4. Is writing important to you? Do you think it will be in the future? What evidence do you have for your answers?
5. How did you feel about your essay before you started it? Did you think you would enjoy it? Did you think it would be hard, or easy? How did you feel about it when you were finished?

To summarize the importance of writing in the correct genre: always keep the audience and their expectations in mind, determine what the purpose of your essay is, and consider what rhetorical effect your writing will have on your reader.

CHAPTER 2

Getting Started

by Moriah Maresh

Developing a Focus/Reading Questions

It is Monday morning. You gaze out of the classroom window while sipping a venti hazelnut latte with double shots of espresso and wonder if there will be time to grab a snack between this class and next, seeing as you skipped breakfast. Suddenly, your sleep-deprived brain snaps to attention as the instructor sets a sheet of paper on your desk. The crisp, bright white dazzles brilliantly in the morning sun, reading: "Argumentative Research Essay." The time has come to write an important essay in first-year writing.

Depending on the specific class and instructor, you may be given a broad prompt or a narrow prompt (i.e., social media vs. the mental health effects of social media). Regardless of the type of prompt, you will need to develop a clear focus, so your research and energy are pushed in the right direction. Let's explore some beneficial steps you can take to effectively develop a focus.

Step One: Understand What you Need to Do

Understanding the assignment is critical. After all, you want your effort to be fruitful and meet all requirements. Be sure to carefully review the assignment multiple times. Let's explore an example of an instructor's assignment sheet together:

Prof. Green
CCSU

Argumentative Research Essay

Social media is prominent in today's world. Whether someone uses social media or not, they are most likely familiar with at least one platform. The presence of these platforms, such as Facebook, Instagram, and Tik-Tok, have revolutionized how, where, and why we interact with friends, family, and strangers. The world has become more connected thanks to social media, but there are also downsides to its development and popularity. This technology is often considered to be a "double-edged sword."

In no less than 1500 words, you will take a stance by arguing whether social media is more beneficial to society or more harmful to society. You must pick a side. While defending your argument, you must include 3+ academic sources. You must also address a counterargument and at least 1 academic source that acknowledges this perspective.

What are the main points to take away from Prof. Green's assignment? Answer these questions:

What is the topic? _____

What are you being asked to do? _____

Is research required? _____

If so, how much? _____

What kind of sources? _____

What is the word requirement? _____

Let's go over your answers:

Prof. Smith
CCSU

Argumentative Research Essay

Social media is prominent in today's world. Whether someone uses social media or not, they are most likely familiar with at least one platform. The presence of these platforms, such as Facebook, Instagram, and Tik-Tok, have revolutionized how, where, and why we interact with friends, family, and strangers. The world has become more connected thanks to social media, but there are also downsides to its development and popularity. The technology is often considered to be a "double-edged sword."

In no less than 1500 words, you will take a stance by arguing whether social media is more beneficial to society or more harmful to society. While defending your argument, you must Include 3+ academic sources. You must also address a counterargument and at least 1 academic source that acknowledges this perspective.

What is the topic? Social Media

What are you being asked to do? Argue whether social media is more helpful than harmful or more harmful than helpful. This means deciding on one side or the other.

Is research required? Yes

If so, how much? 3+ sources for your argument, 1+ for the counterargument

What kind of sources? Academic (see page ## for more information on academic sources)

What is the word requirement? 1500+

Did you get more or less the same responses? If you missed any aspect, consider why that happened. Is there something you did not understand or notice? Did you read too quickly? Did you try to make the assignment something it is not? Again, misinterpreting or misreading assignments can happen. Being sure you fully understand what is required will save your time and energy. Get into the habit of using the questions above to "actively read" your assignment sheets. If you still have questions, don't be afraid to approach your instructor with questions! After all, that is why they are there.

Step Two: Know the Details of the Topic

Once you have a solid grasp of the assignment, let's now dive into the topic we are using as an example: the pros or cons of social media. Taking a stance (also known as taking a position on an arguable issue) can be challenging, regardless of the subject matter. Starting with the simplest technicalities of the topic can help you gauge what you already know. Some questions to consider are:

- What do I know about the topic? _____
- Who is involved in/influenced by this topic? _____
- Where is this topic prevalent? _____
- Why is this topic important/why does it matter? _____

Once you feel confident with the ins-and-outs of the basics, start to think, "What about me?" Turn your thoughts internally. Consider:

- What about this topic interests me?
  - You ideally want to write about something you care about! However, we are not always provided prompts that stir our passion. Reflect on the topic and try to narrow down aspects of it you find intriguing.
  - For example, are you interested in the mental health aspects of social media? Or do you care more about how social media enables professional and social networks on a global scale? Or is there something else?
- What questions come to mind as I think about this topic? What don't you know or understand about this topic? Have you thought about it before?
- What do I want to explore? What would you like to know more about?
  - This doesn't need to be specific. Like in the first question, find a point or several points that catch your attention.

Step Three: Generating Ideas

By this point, you've broken down the assignment to ensure you are responding correctly and considered what you already know about the assigned topic. Now, it's time to develop more precise ideas for your argument. Let's be honest. You might not be passionate about every essay topic assigned during your academic career. However, finding areas you want to explore while remaining true to the prompt will help you develop stronger ideas, write more enthusiastically, and remain focused. Plus, you'll have more fun!

Sticking with Prof. Green's prompt of the pros or cons of social media, let's explore some idea-generating techniques.

Brainstorm

Brainstorming is the practice of developing ideas and approaches that can help you learn more about a topic. Indeed, brainstorming is a great method for exploring ideas to examine and further develop later in the writing process. You want to keep your end goal in mind (see the assignment sheet provided by your instructor!), while at the same time allowing yourself to explore ideas. While there are many kinds of approaches to brainstorming, you can use the following prompts to help kick-start a brainstorming session in first-year writing:

- What is your initial impression of this topic?
- What do you know or understand about this topic?
- What do you not know or understand about this topic?
- What are the positives and negatives of this topic?

- What do you need to do in order to understand more about the topic?
- What makes this topic interesting? To you? To others?

Your responses can be written in an orderly list or a messy, typo-ridden paragraph. You can even scrawl your ideas on post-it notes and arrange them at random on a wall in front of you; afterwards, you can examine the "scattershot" ideas and seek connections and invigorating ideas that would not otherwise have occurred to you. It is important to select a few ideas that seem the most interesting, relevant, and important to you. You can intensify this activity by initiating a new round of brainstorming which builds upon the ideas you have selected as most relevant.

Don't limit yourself to only the methods described in this section of the book, either. There are many approaches to brainstorming you can locate on the Internet and adapt for your own purposes.

Make a List!

Like brainstorming, listing can be beneficial when contemplating a topic. What makes it distinct is that you should write down only words or phrases and not complete sentences. This is because you are looking to make quick connections and associations that you help you make logical connections that can increase your depth of knowledge, develop further questions, and/or create avenues for writing and research later in your writing process.

Listing can be beneficial when contemplating a topic. The process is simple: Make a list! It is essentially brainstorming but in list form. For some people, this format is more effective. Using bullets, write down various points about your broader topic. Then, go back and see which ones interest you most. Try it! Write down ten thoughts that come to mind when you think about our prompt (social media).

- _____
- _____
- _____
- _____
- _____
- _____
- _____
- _____
- _____
- _____

Now let's go over your points. Which are related to each other? Can you form any groups? Which contradict each other? Which interests you the most?

Clustering

Clustering is also known as webbing; rather than putting your ideas into a list, you build an idea cloud on the page. This can allow you to visualize relationships between ideas in ways that are not always visible when we use other pre-writing methods. In the example below, the writer has written down the topic—"ADS"—and circled it. Then the writer has connected ideas related to the topic and developed several potential sub-areas that they could explore further, such as "location" and "messages" (which themselves have points which could be explored or developed in an essay).

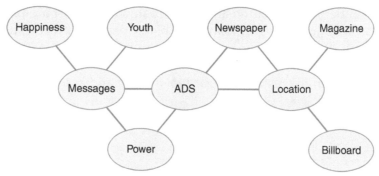

Figure 2.1 An example of clustering
© Kendall Hunt Publishing Company

Freewrite

Freewriting can be very, well, freeing! A lot of students (and instructors) can psych themselves out when developing ideas. Don't let your brain critique your thoughts before you even have them on the page! If you're feeling "writer's block," like your brain went out to lunch, freewriting can help get you back on track. Freewriting is similar to brainstorming. The main difference is that, to freewrite, you need to keep writing! Let those ideas churn, and don't stop the flow. Whatever comes to mind, write it down without judgment, even if that includes "**filler words**" such as "uh," "um," "like," etc. Just write! Consider this example:

I'm not really sure what to argue about social media. Okay. Um. I had coffee this morning with Heather. But that's not about social media. Oh! Heather was cyberbullied on Twitter in high school! That could be a con. Oh, but Zoom lets me Facetime with Ian. So that's a pro. What else? I found a part-time job on Indeed. But some jobs there are fake.

In this case, our writer let her train of thought go wild but never stopped writing when she ran out of ideas. She kept her fingers typing with words like "um" and "okay" until she thought of another point. Never judge when you freewrite!

Another tip: Having a timer going during this writing time can be beneficial. Set a timer for three minutes and try to not stop writing until the timer goes off. Let's try it! Set a timer for three minutes and write whatever comes to mind about the pros or cons of social media. (You may want to use a separate sheet of paper.)

_____

_____

_____

_____

_____

Time's up! Read what you wrote, and circle/highlight points you think are beneficial to your argument or that you can develop further for your paper. Importantly, look for areas that could represent sub-topics within your essay.

Talk it Out

You're not in this alone. Your classmates are in the same boat as you, so why not have discussions about the topic(s)? Brainstorm together! You can also "verbally freewrite," meaning you just talk for a minute or so, either recording yourself or talking to a peer and having them write down what you say. In some classes, the instructor will set aside time for such exercises.

Also, always remember: Pay attention and participate in class discussions. This is a helpful way to develop ideas without sitting in front of a blank page and trying to do it all on your own. You can (and should!) take the time to write to your professor, or visit during office hours, with questions and observations from your pre-writing. These interactions can help consolidate, solidify, and/or deepen the results of your pre-writing and assist as you begin composing your essay.

Know the Rhetorical Situation

Consider the **Rhetorical Situation.** Let's return (?) to our graphic:

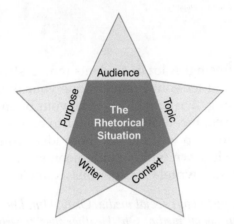

Figure 2.2 The Rhetorical Situation
© *Kendall Hunt Publishing Company*

Keeping our social media topic in mind, what information could you include in each part of the star?

Writer (What do I know? What do I bring to the conversation?)

_____

Audience (This is for a writing class in a university. So, who is my audience?)

_____

Topic (What specific aspects of social media do I want to explore?)

_____

Purpose (Yes, I was assigned this paper. However, what do I want to accomplish with it?)

_____

Context (In what circumstances am I writing? What year? What country? etc.)

_____

Cognitive Strategies

Cognitive Strategies, or how people solve problems and learn, help you strategize to learn more effectively and reach your goal. There are many different strategies you can employ, such as:

Set goals

What do you want to accomplish? Do you want a draft completed by Friday? Do you want your research completed next Monday? How many words do you need? Are you close to the requirements? Having specific goals provides you with various end points throughout the writing process and helps you acknowledge your progress.

Indicate what you already know

Give yourself credit! You will accumulate a lot of information during the writing process, but acknowledge the information *you* bring to the topic! For example, what have been your experiences with social media? Think of a time you experienced something positive or negative. What was that experience? What happened? What were the implications of that experience? This is you bringing your own information–as a **primary source**–to the conversation.

Indicate what you do not know

Part of the writing process is research, and, in order to do research, you need to have questions to answer. What questions do you have about your topic? What do you not know but want to know? Once you recognize what ideas need developing, you can use your curiosity to nourish those areas and grow them into an intriguing essay.

Connect the Dots

Did you ever play "Connect the Dots" as a kid, when you traced numbered dots in order until a picture appeared? A similar "game" can be played when piecing together ideas. Do you see connections between one concept and another in your topic? Do you notice trends? To utilize this strategy, you may find it helpful to create charts or graphs to map out any connections you see. For example:

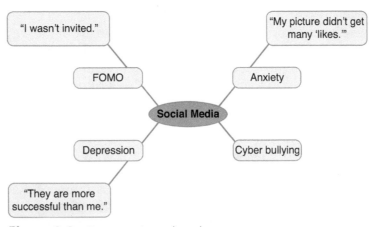

Figure 2.3 Connecting the dots
© *Kendall Hunt Publishing Company*

The above "idea spider" illustrates how various ideas are related to social media. However, how are the ideas related to each other? Also, why does this matter? You want the reader to *care* about your topic. So, you need to illustrate why they should! Considering some of the ideas above, let's think about how they could be woven together:

> Example 1: "Social media is negative because it causes mental health problems. This should be taken seriously."
>
> Does this really give a reader any reasons why they should believe the author or take the argument seriously? No.
>
> Example 2: "Social media is negative because it presents a platform for bullying. Cyberbullying can cause mental health problems like depression and anxiety." This is much more specific and thorough while providing reasons why the reader should care.

Your reader needs to understand why they should take time out of their day to consider your argument. Readers only read the words you put on the page. They cannot read your mind. Therefore, connect the dots for them!

Let's try it. Write two or three sentences connecting the dots between these ideas: social media, friendship, and memories. You can write on either side of our topic (positive or negative). If you want to create a graphic to help you, use the blank space provided before writing your sentences on the lines below.

_____

_____

_____

_____

Recognize what you need clarified

You've brought a lot of ideas to the table. You've set goals. You've answered questions. Now, what do you not quite understand? Pay attention to your uncertainties, whether they pertain to the assignment itself, a piece of data, or your own reasoning. Think of this as the time to "wash the windows." If any part of your writing process is murky or hazy, now is the time to polish and clear it up. If you, the writer, are confused, your audience will be, too. Make the windows to your ideas shine!

Narrow Down the Topic

In this chapter, you have been introduced to (or reminded of!) many of the ways in which a writer can develop ideas on a topic. The trick is to allow yourself the freedom to explore while at the same time remaining focused on the topic. You want to figure out what you know, what you are interested in, and what you need to know more about. Pre-writing activities and conversations with classmates and instructors in your class are crucial tools to help develop your thinking on a particular topic.

At this point, you should begin refining or narrowing your topic as you enter the next stage in your process. Ask yourself is there a particular area within a topic that strikes you as interesting, or about which you had more to say, or about which you believe there will be ample resources for writing and research? Check your discoveries against the assignment sheet and expectations of your instructor, who is available for consultation. Do you have the right idea? Is there a need to add to, subtract from, or otherwise adapt what you have discovered during pre-writing in order to have the right kind of focus? This kind of "course correction" is not unusual; in fact, it is a good idea to occasionally "zoom out" of your process to make sure you are still pursuing a focused path, and then to make any calibrations needed.

Conclusion

We have explored various techniques to help us get started with writing, but there are plenty of other techniques out there. You can learn more by visiting the campus Writing Center or going online to Purdue Owl. If we covered every idea for getting started, we would need much more time than a single chapter! The methods discussed, as well as many others, can be beneficial for many types of writing (see the chapter on **genre**.) So, whether you are a chemistry major or a history major, these methods can be of help! The more you practice incorporating them into your writing process, the more effective and natural they will become.

CHAPTER 3

Writing Processes

by Samantha Seamans

Organizing

Gathering Your Resources

Your professor may have given you an assignment to help you practice your writing abilities. In a previous chapter, we used the example of social media as a topic and then used pre-writing strategies to develop ideas on that topic. After you develop a stronger sense of the topic, you are likely to write a more formal, graded assignment that involves research. One such example is the **annotated bibliography**. In this assignment, you batch together several related sources in the required citation format, organize alphabetically by author last name, and provide a critical summary of each source. Here are two examples:

Sample MLA Annotation

Austin, James P. "Traversing Academic Contexts: An Egyptian Writer's Literacy Learning Trajectory From Public School to Transnational University." *Written Communication*, vol. 39, no. 4, Oct. 2022, pp. 630–58. *EBSCOhost*, https://doi.org/10.1177/07410883221114085.

Austin presents original research that tracks the academic writing development of a single person: Farah, a female Egyptian student who matriculates from the Egyptian public school system to an elite transnational university that is located within Egypt, but which uses English as its primary language, and which adopts an U.S. educational model. To assist with this research, Austin presents histories of the Egyptian public schooling system, which tends to exert strict expectations for topic selection ad attitude expression in school writing, and the transnational university, which promotes western-style critical thinking and questioning of authority. Austin finds that Farah appropriates so-called western approaches to both develop her writing and pursue research into an Islamic charity organization which serves the Egyptian public interest.

Sample APA Annotation

Austin, J. P. (2022). Traversing academic contexts: An Egyptian writer's literacy learning trajectory from public school to transnational university. *Written Communication*, *39*(4), 630–658. https://doi.org/10.1177/07410883221114085

Austin presents original research that tracks the academic writing development of a single person: Farah, a female Egyptian student who matriculates from the Egyptian public school system to an elite transnational university that is located within Egypt, but which uses English as its primary language, and which adopts an U.S. educational model. To assist with this research, Austin presents histories of the Egyptian public schooling system, which tends to exert strict expectations for topic selection ad attitude expression in school writing, and the transnational university, which promotes western-style critical thinking and questioning of authority. Austin finds that Farah appropriates so-called western approaches to both develop her writing and pursue research into an Islamic charity organization which serves the Egyptian public interest.

Source: James Austin

A complete annotated bibliography includes as many sources as required by your instructor, presented in alphabetical order. Your instructor may also have specific instructions for the kinds of annotations they would like to see. This assignment can help you find credible sources to support (and test) the points you are developing on the topic.

Exercise

Genres, Getting Started, and Engaging With Sources all have helpful tips on what to do when reflecting on, developing a focus and/or summarizing our sources, and how you take notes is relative to these processes. On a separate sheet of paper, or if you have a hard copy of your primary source that you don't mind marking up (or you can use pencils and sticky notes), read through your secondary source and begin to identify the who, what, when, where, why and how:

- Who is the author? What do you know about them? Do they have the qualifications to seem credible on this topic?
- What is the main point? Look in the abstract and introductory matter for a thesis.
- How recent is this source? Is it too old to be relevant today?
- Where is it published? Is that venue credible and appropriate?
- Why has this been written? Is it in response to another writer, or in reaction to a pressing issue in the world? Or something else?
- How does it develop its thesis? What are its methods and/or evidence?

Your instructor may have more specific versions of these questions or may focus on some of them more than others. Still, the questions above should provide you with a good approach to reading and evaluating a secondary source that can fit well with the expectations of your CCSU writing instructor.

What is important here is that you can readily identify the basics of your secondary source at any time throughout the writing process. If you can do this, then you have a good, working knowledge of your source and can easily identify within other secondary sources, and so on, what information is most relative and supportive toward the purpose and intent of your discussion moving forward.

Choosing a Focus

Once you have completed an annotated bibliography (or any other critical source evaluation assignment or activity), you should be in better position to narrow your focus further.

If you have not done so already (please refer to the chapter on Getting Started), you will need to narrow the focus of your conversation by choosing one response to the assignment that fits with the instructor's expectations. If you are still unsure of which direction to take, consult the chapter on Genres for a discussion on how to approach particular topics. If your instructor has not already assigned a genre, many times, choosing a genre will help you settle on a direction. This response will become your "working" thesis. For example:

In reference to Sherman Alexie's essay, "The Joy of Reading and Writing: Superman and Me":

Initial question: "Who are Sherman Alexie's heroes in his essay, 'The Joy of Reading and Writing: Superman and Me'"?

Working thesis: "In 'The Joy of Reading and Writing: Superman and Me' by Sherman Alexie, Alexie's heroes are his father who loved to read, Superman who taught him to read and his students who have broken down the barriers."

Remember: While you have chosen a focus and put it in sentence form, your working thesis will change and become more refined as your conversation develops. This means that the essentials will stay the same, your main topic "Alexie's heroes" and your subtopics, "his father," "Superman" and "his students," however the order of your subtopics (path) may change, and the supporting details will become more specific as the process of writing your essay is completed.

When you feel confident in choosing which response you would like to have a conversation with your reader about, now you need to get your initial thoughts about your chosen topic down on paper and decide on a path.

Drafting

While we all have a different perspective on any given topic, our common goal is to respond appropriately and effectively to the topic. A first draft is an essential tool for organizing and clarifying your thoughts, and to receive feedback for revision *before* you submit an essay for a grade.

First Draft

The first draft of an essay is always the most exploratory. While you are organizing and developing your draft to the best of your ability, you are also experimenting by trying things out. Should your body paragraphs be organized in this way, or another way? Are these the best points to make? Do you have enough evidence to support your main points? Is it specific enough? Have you developed your paragraphs to the best of your ability? The truth is that we may have a sense of our responses to these questions but through a first draft we put these questions (and others) to the test. By the time you complete a first draft, you should be able to critically review what you have written and gain a greater sense of the essay's strengths as well as where it needs further development.

When you review your draft, or when you do a peer review of other students' writing, try engaging first with what we call "higher order concerns"—areas such as the focus, organization, and development of the essay. Consider these questions:

- Do you maintain the correct focus throughout, or are there lapses?
- Is this focus appropriate for the assignment?
- Is the essay organized logically?
- Are paragraphs developed appropriately, with topic sentences, evidence, and explanation that ties evidence to the essay's focus?

In a first draft, responses to these questions are likely to highlight areas of focus for future drafts. This is why the drafting process is so powerful in academic writing, because you will notice through early drafts areas that you need to improve upon. By taking the time to improve upon them *before submitting the work for a final grade*, you are improving the essay. This will show your instructor that you have learned more about the topic and the way to develop an academic essay. And this will often result in improved marks.

Overall, the purpose of your first draft is to recognize how your perspective on the topic will guide you toward the focus of your conversation about the topic. This means that, as you are drafting, you are also striving to meet the assignment focus. How can you do that?

Here is one example:

When reading Sherman Alexie's "The Joy of Reading and Writing: Superman and Me," there are several topics that can be discussed, such as Native American life on a reservation, educational opportunities for Native Americans, superheroes, and racism to name a few. If your instructor has asked you to write about Alexie's superheroes, you have some additional choices to make as Alexie introduces several. In this example, we outline some common steps towards understanding what a superhero is and then how to apply those qualities attributed to a superhero to Alexie's text. Doing this will help us more readily identify the superheroes in Alexie's text. Here is one approach:

1. Begin with a clear understanding of what a superhero is. Your instructor may have given you a definition to work with, you may have workshopped a definition in class, or you have found a definition (or two) that combined, best describes the qualities of a superhero within the context of your primary source.

2. Use that definition to search for qualities within the text of a superhero and note who or what those qualities are being used to describe. Here is how it works:

If the definition you are using states "a well-meaning and kindly character who possesses extraordinary abilities and acts voluntarily for the service of others who are in need, whether an individual, a group, or a community," you can begin by looking for characters who "possess extraordinary abilities." In the text, Alexie's father "went to Catholic school on purpose." With some preliminary research, you will soon find that his father attending Catholic school on purpose was a brave and purposeful act, because when Alexie's father was growing up in the 1940's–50's, Indian children on reservations were still being forced to attend boarding schools which stripped them of their culture, language and essentially any identity they possessed relating to being Indigenous Americans. If Alexie's father went *on purpose*, this means he *had a purpose*. Dad possessed the *extraordinary* ability, at a very young age, to confront cultural hostility with the intent of changing things for himself, his family and his community on the reservation.

In keeping with this example, once you have made this connection about Alexie's father you can begin to locate other areas of the text where his father's heroism is explicitly referenced, implied, or commented upon. This material will assist you in composing your first draft.

Second Draft

A second draft should refine and clarify any of the "higher order concerns" addressed in the section on writing a first draft and should begin devoting attention to the "lower order concerns" that we observe at the sentence level. A common way forward is to view your second draft as the first step towards clarifying your main topic and developing your supporting evidence (subtopics). There are two distinctive approaches towards writing an academic essay. One continues from what you have practiced throughout high school, which takes a more organic approach and develops a conversation "as it comes". The second is more of a "divide and conquer" approach, which takes separate components of an essay and develops them separately. Whichever way comes naturally to you, all writers will need to consider, at some point, how well each component of their essay works together to best fulfill your (the writer's) intent.

Know Your Audience

It is important when beginning your second draft to become increasingly aware of your audience. Since you are writing an essay for academic practice and not necessarily for pleasure (first draft), it is at this point you need to begin to consider what an academic audience will expect. For this reason, you will need to be aware of format (both page and essay), word choice and intent. Whether your general writing process is "as it comes" or "divide and conquer," being aware of the format of an academic essay can help you speak to your audience in a more clear and intentional way.

Moving Beyond the Baseline

As a beginning college writer, you come to this next step in your academic journey with your own personal writing process. Most have had practice writing five paragraph essays (intro, three subtopics, close) and in writing these essays, we often begin with an introduction. What happens more times than not is that our focus becomes about the introduction, because of how we have been taught to write introductions, and not about the inclusion and/or the development of our subtopics. In relative terms, our writing journey up and through high school has served us well and has allowed us to include the basic information that we need within an essay. Now, as we have taken in all that we needed from high school and move into our next level of academia, we need to expand our scope not only in learning about new topics and how to better utilize resources, but we also need to include more clear and relative information in what we give back—each in its own designated space. This also helps as we continue with a second draft, where we are targeting areas that we have identified as requiring additional attention.

One way to begin your second draft should is with a copy and paste of your first draft into a new file. This way as you get to editing and you find later that you would like to refer to the original, you will still have your first draft on file. You can always delete earlier drafts after publication or at the end of the semester when you will be moving on to different material. This also means that you will be working within the draft to develop areas from the first draft you have identified as in need of improvement.

In the past when we began each draft with an introduction, each time we went back to revise a draft, we often read from the beginning to a point that needed revising. Then back to the beginning to the next point that needed revising. This approach tends to bring "diminishing returns," for not only is it inefficient, but it also becomes less effective the more it is used.

As you work within your draft, consider feedback or reflection on the first draft. Are there areas within paragraphs that are not quite focused appropriately? For instance, does the introduction include all the "moves" one would expect, resulting in a specific, clear statement of focus? Do body paragraphs support that focus through their organization and development? Do you develop enough reasons to support that focus? Are body paragraphs organized in the correct order, or should they be reorganized?

As you respond to questions such as these, you may find that your thinking on the topic changes—sometimes a little, sometimes a lot. As you revise, you can always loop back around to the focus in the introduction and refine what you write there, in order to bring it into line with what you are developing in the revised body paragraphs.

Editing for a Second Draft

A tool you may want to consider while editing your work goes by several names; "the power of three," "rule of three," "the magic of three," and surely several more. However you may choose to refer to this theory, the point here is that it is commonly believed that the human brain can grasp ideas or concepts grouped in trios. Throughout history, some of the most popular mainstream references have come to us in three's; Father, Son, and Holy Ghost; before, during, and after; introduction, climax, and resolution; Snap! Crackle! Pop! This psychological theory is so well known that it is a common tool used in mainstream marketing, storytelling and even home decorating.

In applying this rule to essay writing, you can now see more readily the three main components to your essay, three main components to your paragraphs and in some cases, three components within your sentence structure. Now that you have been introduced to the "rule of three," don't be surprised at how many 3's you will see!

Here is how the "rule of three" can potentially work for you:

An idea to consider when you are preparing to edit your second draft is that the *process* of editing your work is different from the presentation of your work. What this means is that, in contrast to how we commonly present a topic within an essay; introduction, subtopics, and closing, *you can edit each area in any order you like*. To highlight the areas that need more editing, one approach is to introduce essay structure and paragraph structure when preparing to edit your second draft.

First, as you become more familiar with the components of an academic essay; introduction, subtopics, and closing, and as you engage with the copy/paste of your first draft, you may begin to see more clearly what you have available to use from your first draft, what you do not need, and what you need to add. These are your areas of focus.

After you have placed what you have so far into the areas where they would best serve your discussion, then you can apply to each area the structure of a paragraph; topic, evidence, explanation, transition. Now you will be able to see what you have available, and what you need to include to continue to complete the scaffolding of your second draft. This will allow you to work within paragraphs to target those areas in greatest need of revision.

Your choice of which component to work on first should depend on which components have the most impact on the essay. You have already put together your working thesis, which will keep you focused on your main topic and your preliminary subtopics. The next logical step may be to work on developing each of those subtopics separately, since it is their job to support your overall claim.

Setting Up Your Second Draft

Because, for now, you are setting aside your introduction and closing to be worked on independently, imagine you are moving your introduction and closing off screen to revisit later. In fact, academic writers will sometimes cut and paste their introduction and conclusion to the bottom of their essay and move them to the second page. This way you cannot forget about them as they are still visible, but they are far enough out of your direct line of vision to become a distraction during the editing of your second draft.

With your introduction and conclusion out of the way, your working thesis becomes an essential feature in your work moving forward. For this reason, placing your working thesis into the most predominant space in your developing essay, into your title space (yes, centering it as well!), can help reinforce the importance of the focus of your discussion. If you keep your focus in the forefront, you will be less likely to drift off topic as you develop your subtopics and move further down the page away from that title space. It is also easier to revisit that focus and refine it as necessary.

Next, take a look at your working thesis and see which subtopics you have written about in your first draft. Begin with the one that interests you the most or the one with the most information transferred from your first draft. This way, you can begin the process more easily and get the hang of what you need for each subtopic before you need to potentially do more research.

As you read through the body paragraphs, use the organization of the paragraph as a way to check for sufficient development. For example, do topic sentences express logical relationships of what has come before? Do they express exactly what the paragraph will be about, and how this contributes to your focus? How about our evidence? Are you providing quotations as necessary, and/or specific paraphrases, which clearly belong to the paragraphs where they are located? Are you able to clearly link that evidence to your focus? At each step along the body paragraphs, there is an opportunity to further focus and develop your essay in the areas that need the most attention. At the same time, you have the opportunity to revisit and refine your focus as you write.

Subtopics

As stated above, subtopics often come in sets of three. Think of the relationship between a main topic and subtopics in an essay like the different components of a free-standing table—you need a minimum of three legs to evenly support a tabletop. (fig. a) Tables come in all shapes and sizes, but with only one or two legs, the tabletop will not be equally supported and can topple when too much weight is placed on one or the other side of the tabletop. In opposition, a tabletop will stand firmly with more than three legs, especially a very large table (a thesis or dissertation) where four legs will add more even support. (fig. b). Just keep in mind that with the more legs you add past four, the greater the possibility that they are decorative and perhaps not essential. That is to say: make some clear choices about the sub-topics which find most worthy of inclusion in your essay. (fig. c)

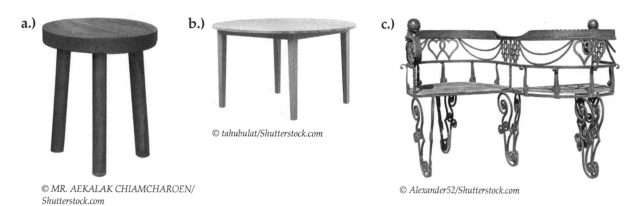

a.)

© MR. AEKALAK CHIAMCHAROEN/
Shutterstock.com

b.)

© tahubulat/Shutterstock.com

c.)

© Alexander52/Shutterstock.com

When writing about a subtopic in a five-paragraph essay, each subtopic commonly follows this basic format for a body paragraph: paragraph:

- Topic sentence: introducing the topic of the paragraph
- 3-5 developmental sentences: providing evidence in the support of examples from the text, outside statistics, etc., plus explanations which contextualize the evidence by explaining how it supports the topic sentence and therefore the essay's main focus
- Transitional sentence (optional): bringing your reader from the current subtopic to the next subtopic. This sometime occurs in topic sentences at the beginning of new paragraphs instead of at the conclusion of a preceding paragraph.

Each subtopic will also include the same basic scaffolding of an academic essay, "I make this claim, because of this evidence." The key here is to focus on the subtopic itself. Many times, we can show the relationship between a subtopic and a topic just by describing the subtopic. For example:

In the essay "Mystic Pizza" by Pauline Philips, the main topic of her essay is her favorite food, pizza. Notice how the introductory sentence of her first subtopic introduces the subtopic of *crust* and relates it to her main topic of *pizza*, while her developmental sentences only focus on the crust itself:

> After a topic sentence in which Philips describes crispy crust as an ideal end to a piece of pizza, the writer continues:
>
> *In fact, many people consider the outer crust of a pizza to be the best part of each slice. Some people even go so far as to save all of their crusts until they have finished eating each portion of toppings just so they can savor all of the crusts at once. Others even go further by developing a system for eating their crusts by first removing and eating each soft, warm center before devouring the crispy, crunchy outer edges. While the crust is high in the overall top five of favorite pizza components, for me, cheese runs a very close second. (Philips 1)*

In one respect, a body paragraph is a self-contained unit consisting of one topic. These paragraphs function in concert to support the overall focus of the essay; any body paragraph which is weaker than the others therefore will lessen the effectiveness of the entire essay. This is why it is crucial to make sure your body paragraphs, and the sub-topics developed therein, are appropriate for the focus of the essay you are writing, are appropriately organized, and are adequately developed. These three factors will determine the effectiveness of the paragraphs.

Likewise, you will want to make sure that the order in which you present the body paragraphs expresses a logical relationship between the sub-topics. For example, should you organize sub-topics from least to most important, or the other way around? Or do they occur in a logical sequence where one follows from o is caused by the subtopics preceding it? Giving this high quality of attention to the overall development of the essay is a critical and attainable way to "step up" the quality of your writing in ways your instructors are sure to notice.

Sometimes, a subtopic for an essay can contain many paragraphs. For example, in Philips' essay we see three clear subtopics: crust, cheese, and vegetables. Each of these subtopics has at least one paragraph each with the exception of subtopic 3, vegetables, which has two paragraphs. The first paragraph discussing vegetables as a whole and the second paragraph discussing onions.

The essay follows the same pattern of "I make this claim, because of this evidence." Importantly, these also show how some sub-topics are more complex or have sub-areas of their own which require additional development. These essays show how can develop more complex sub-topics within the original framework of the 5-paragraph essay. Indeed, as you take on more complex writing tasks, you will find yourself adapting more basic approaches to meet more complex expectations.

Introductions and Closings

A common misconception we learn in high school is that introductions for a traditional English class are like every other paragraph we include in our essays. This is true, in some respects, for an introduction is a paragraph: it begins with a topic sentence, includes developmental sentences and a transition. In many ways, however, introductions are unique. The purpose of an introductory paragraph is to introduce the main topic of the entire essay. In other words, an introduction paragraph and the sentences within perform double duty. Not only do they identify themselves as a paragraph, but in doing so, identify things to come in the essay itself. We can almost think of the introductory paragraph as the topic sentence of the entire essay.

Even when you are writing for another discipline such as History or the Social Sciences, where your thesis statement comes at the beginning of your introduction rather than the end, it is still important to consider the question, how can we write an introduction for a topic that we have barely yet written about? For this reason, a *working* thesis statement that includes our initial topic and intent is enough for us to begin writing our supporting paragraphs. Just do not get stuck on needing a "fully developed" thesis statement or introduction before you begin developing the rest of your conversation. A final introduction tends to arrive once we know what we are introducing: the rest of the essay.

For this reason, writing your full introduction after you have written the body of your essay will help you write an introduction that will clearly introduce your subject matter based on the information you have come to know and depend on to support your claims, because you have taken the time, first, to get to know and to develop your main topic through your subtopics.

This means that if it is part of your process to write an introduction for your first draft, consider setting that information aside, after you have gotten your creative juices flowing, until after you have developed the main body of your conversation. When you have done so, consider the following as a way to "pick-up" where you left off.

In a high school English class, many of us have been taught to write an introduction with the following components:

1. An opening hook to catch the reader's attention.
   a. This can include a relevant quotation, a question/example, a narrative or anecdotal opening, or even a position opposing your own
2. Relevant background information that the reader needs to know.
   a. For example, what is the topic you are writing about? What is your purpose? What context does a general reader need to understand what follows? The answers to these questions may appear on the assignment sheets provided by our instructor. They may have been discussed in class. Or you may be able to find this information by visiting your instructor's office during office hours.
3. A thesis statement that presents your main point or argument.
   a. As before, think of your thesis as a claim with reasons: I think X because of these reasons. The reasons will likely correspond to the sub-topics you are developing in the body paragraphs. This approach helps to "seal" the introduction to what comes after.

Let's compare each of the elements to each of the basic components of a general paragraph:

A hook to catch the reader's attention = (introduce your topic) topic sentence
of the paragraph

Information the reader needs to know = (develop your topic) Developmental sentences

A thesis statement = (main topic, purpose, and subtopics) — literally, "I make this claim, because of this evidence," which is a transition from the current topic to the next topic

In considering the first body paragraph of "Mystic Pizza," we can see that it has a topic sentence:

"Every person has their favorites; favorite sports team, favorite basketball player, favorite friend, favorite vacation spot, favorite quiet place, favorite food" (Philips 1 p.1).

This topic sentence in the first body paragraph includes the topic of the paragraph, *crust*, and other specific word choices reflecting the main thread to her essay, *perfect*, and Philips' favorite food, *pizza*. Similarly, a topic sentence for the introduction would also seek to hook the reader with an interesting opener and stablishing the topic for the entire essay.

In considering introductions to both body paragraphs and introductions, we can more clearly see that the topic sentence for an introduction works for the entire essay while the topic sentence for the first body paragraph establishes the subject of the first paragraph only. This is an important distinction, for it tells us that the introduction has a big job to do in setting up the entire essay. It is much easier and more effective to complete your introduction after you have fully developed your body paragraphs. Even with common threads woven throughout the essay through word choice, the introductory paragraph of an essay has a much wider scope than the body paragraphs of an essay. Because the body paragraphs tend to be more focused, this would be where the information *for* your introduction will ultimately come from. It only makes sense to write your introduction separately and after you have developed your body paragraphs.

In the meantime, here are some easy tips for writing your introduction:

1. Remember that your introduction is a paragraph, so make sure you have a complete paragraph: a topic sentence, several developmental sentences, and a transition from the current topic to the next topic. Your goal is to interest your reader, provide context, and present a specific focus.

2. Write your topic sentence to perform double duty by not only introducing the topic of the entire essay, but also appealing to a wide audience.

3. Use your developmental sentences to provide the "must know" broader strokes such as defining terms to provide context and/or show a pattern of thought that leads you to your thesis statement.

4. Follow that same pattern of "I make this claim, because of this evidence" and literally use this pattern to help you formulate your working thesis statement: *"My favorite food is pizza, because of the crust, cheese and vegetables"* (Philips 1).

5. Remember that your thesis statement is a transition from the current topic (favorite food is pizza) to the next topic/s (crust, cheese, vegetables).

    Be sure to understand the discipline you are writing for, meaning that an academic audience expects the thesis to come at the end of your introduction.

In a typical WRT class, closings are essentially written in reverse order of the introduction. While the sentences may need to be adjusted for grammatical purposes, traditionally, the first sentence of a closing is the thesis statement followed by the developmental sentences. These sentences together represent your main point.

Exercise

To encourage your reader to reflect on your conversation with interest within your conclusion, consider providing them the opportunity to understand the broader importance of your main idea. On a separate sheet of paper:

1. Begin with a summary of your main point. This can be accomplished through the practice of paraphrasing.

2. After you have summarized, what details can you add to better develop and clarify your main point?

When you feel you have clearly expressed your main point, you should leave your reader with something to think about on their own. In "Mystic Pizza", Philips' essay ends with a question: "What's your favorite?" (2 p.6). Usually, essays don't end with a question, and if your instructor would rather you end your essay without one, then turn the question into a statement: "Everyone has a favorite". While you are not directly asking your reader to answer a question, you are still leaving your reader with something that encourages further thought. Here are some options that you might include after your main point to encourage your reader to act. Check any or all options that you may use in your conclusion:

- Identify the significance of your topic for issues in the "real world"
- Suggest solutions or changes for the future; offer a prediction
- Ask a rhetorical question that encourages the reader to keep thinking about your topic
- End with a relevant quotation that reflects your main ideas
- Call for more research on your topic

This approach of adding something new in the conclusion will help make your essay more effective because you are taking advantage of the unique qualities of the conclusion to "cinch" your case. After all, you have presented your case and ideally, made a convincing case. The conclusion is your opportunity to close the deal. It also shows your instructor that you are being thorough and taking every opportunity to write an effective essay.

Proofreading

College is challenging. Managing your time between work, classes, homework and a social life, there are a lot of new challenges for first year college students especially. One such challenge is the development of academic habits that will help you thrive in your classes; in WRT classes, the development of a durable and adaptable writing process is key to your success. We have discussed much about the writing process in this chapter. In this final section, we will discuss proofreading, an important aspect of the writing process that should come near the end of the process, prior to submission. Addressing these "lower order concerns" at the sentence level makes sense once you feel satisfied about your focus, organization, and development.

As with all aspects of the writing process, proofreading near will help establish you as a credible and reputable communicator on the topic you are writing about. Reputable sources know how to:

- **Spell**. Spelling is essential for a reputable source, so just like you don't allow your sources to speak for you, don't let autocorrect spell for you.
- **Write in complete sentences**. Notice I did not say proper sentences, just complete sentences. Much gibberish can be spoken without any help from your computer. If you cannot put a sentence together, your reader will see your confusion.
- **"Massage" their language**. Be as clear as you can. Many times, we know what we want to say, but for some reason just can't get it down on paper. Reputable sources give it more than one try over a period of time.
- **Walk away**. Give your thoughts time to settle. The subconscious is this wonderous little internal part of our brain that keeps thinking even though we are unaware. The great part is that in about 12–24 hours it will help us improve the existing language in our essay. How easy is that!

Incorporating proofreading into your writing process will not only allow you to see your own missteps but will encourage you to take ownership of your claims while building confidence in your ability to communicate more clearly.

A common aspect of proofreading involves understanding sentence boundaries in writing. I say "in writing" to emphasize the difference between writing and speaking. After all, we often speak in run-ons and sentence fragments. The patterns of informal speech are usually very different from that of formal academic writing. This is why it is a good idea to read your essay out loud, searching for areas where the language may be read as more informal and, as such, not quite right for the situation. Below is a tutorial that can help assist with sentence boundary challenges that may appear in your academic writing.

Comma Splice/Fused/Fragments

A fused sentence incorrectly joins two independent clauses with no punctuation; consequently, the reader doesn't know where one thought ends and another begins.

<u>Peter brought a bologna sandwich for lunch</u> <u>he forgot to bring me one</u>.
<u>This new dress makes me look sallow</u> <u>I will have to return it</u>.
<u>Kimberly got new glasses</u> <u>everyone complimented her on them</u>.

A comma splice incorrectly joins two independent clauses with a comma.

<u>Peter brought a bologna sandwich for lunch,</u> <u>he forgot to bring me one</u>.
<u>This new dress makes me look sallow,</u> <u>I will have to return it</u>.
<u>Kimberly got new glasses,</u> <u>everyone complimented her on them</u>.

A fragment occurs when one or more of the key elements of a sentence (independent clause) is missing: subject, verb, or complete idea.

Because Peter forgot to bring a bologna sandwich for me.
This new dress making me look sallow.
Since Kimberly got new glasses.

<u>**Fused sentences and comma splices can be corrected in several ways:**</u>

1. **Make two separate sentences by using a period:**
   Peter brought a bologna sandwich for lunch. He forgot to bring me one.

2. **Use a comma and coordinating conjunction—FANBOYS = for, and, nor, but, or, yet, so:**
   Peter brought a bologna sandwich for lunch, but he forgot to bring me one.

3. **Use a subordinating conjunction—because, although, unless, when, if, since…:**
   Although Peter brought a bologna sandwich for lunch, he forgot to bring me one.

4. **Use a semicolon and conjunctive adverb—THINTIC = therefore, however, indeed, nevertheless, in fact, consequently:**
   Peter brought a bologna sandwich for lunch; however, he forgot to bring me one.

<u>**Fragments can be corrected in several ways:**</u>

1. **If the fragment gives information that applies to another sentence in the paragraph, join the fragment with it.**
   Because Peter forgot to bring a bologna sandwich for me. I didn't have lunch. Because Peter forgot to bring a bologna sandwich for me, I didn't have lunch.

2. **Add missing elements or change the form of existing words to make a complete sentence.**
   This new dress making me look sallow. This new dress makes me look sallow.

3. **Delete words that make the fragment a dependent clause.**
   Since Kimberly got new glasses. Kimberly got new glasses.

Peer Review

The key to a successful peer review is to offer **constructive** feedback. By constructive, we mean useful, practical, worthwhile, beneficial, encouraging and above all, positive in tone. Did you ever hear the phrase "it's not what you say, it's how you say it"? Now is the time to practice "it". Your instructor has likely provided you with information and/or other expectations for your peer review; you should always follow the lead of your instructor where peer review is concerned. You can also use the aspects of the writing process to guide your approach to peer review (and to read and interpret the peer review you receive from others): how well focused is the draft? How well organized and developed is it? It is important in peer review to describe what you read but also to make some qualitative evaluation—albeit kindly!—which will allow your peer to understand what areas you read as well done, and which areas could use additional attention.

Often, it is not the positive feedback that is lacking. In fact, in many cases there is an abundance of positive feedback such as "great job," "I like this," or "great example," but without any specifics to back them up. Peer review is similar to what we are all doing while writing an essay: "I make this claim, because of this evidence," so don't leave out the evidence!

During daily life and especially while we are learning, positive reinforcement helps us discover new paths and establish boundaries for ourselves and for others. However, in the case of learning, we really need to know specifically what we did right (or wrong for that matter) so we can build confidence in our communication skills. What "job" did I do and why was it "great"? What especially did you "like" about that sentence? What was so "great" about the example I used? Even though it makes us feel better when someone agrees with us or gives us a shout- out for being especially brilliant, we still need to know why, so we can either do it, or not do it, again. In listening to others talk about our habits, we can in turn learn about ourselves and improve on or do away with these habits. In our mind's eye, we are always the hardest to see, therefore we need the advice of others when it comes to better communicating with others. Keep these tips in mind:

- **Be patient**. Remember that what may be obvious to you may not be obvious to someone else.
- **Approach with an open mind**. Opinions differ, and it is your job as a reviewer to approach a topic from the point of clarity. This means that you ask yourself "is the author's claim clear and is there clear evidence to back that claim?"
- **Do not judge**. Opinions differ as well as educational backgrounds and abilities. It is not our place to judge. It is only our place to look for clarity - do we understand the claim and is the evidence offered relevant to that claim - then to point out areas where clarity can be improved.
- **Be constructive**. Let your peers know when something is clear and briefly tell them why. If something is not clear, kindly indicate where the message is unclear with "I am not sure what you are saying here. Perhaps a different word choice would help."
- **Be kind**. Above all else, kindness goes a long way. Many seemingly discouraging criticisms have been delivered in a kind way and been received as encouraging. As long as the message is constructive in nature and positive in tone.
- **The process is different from the presentation**. What this means is that even though the end result of a writing project should be conversational, the process of building that conversation is quite different from the presentation. Academic conversations are not spontaneous. They take research, thought, patience and a keen understanding of your audience. Be aware of this process not only in your own writing, but especially in peer review. Give suggestions that will help your peer see where they need to clarify through more research, thought, patience, understanding, relatability and review.

Interpreting Feedback

Feedback, in many ways, is not comprehensive. In fact, the further you get into your college career and beyond, the less comprehensive feedback is going to be, so now is the time to take full advantage of what you will get.

- **Be patient** with others and with yourself. Remember that what may be obvious to someone else may not be obvious to you. Give yourself permission to learn from observation, practice, and review.
- **Approach with an open mind**. Opinions differ, and it is your job as a writer to approach a topic from the point of clarity. This means that you ask yourself "is my claim clear and is there clear evidence to back that claim?" If your reviewer's feedback contradicts this, take their outside point of view into consideration before you dismiss it or change the direction of your conversation.
- **Do not judge**. Opinions differ as well as educational backgrounds and abilities. It is not our place to judge. It is only our place to look for clarity - do we understand the feedback and is the evidence offered relevant to that feedback - then we can begin to develop and refine those areas where clarity can be improved.
- **Be constructive** with your approach to feedback. Your reviewer should let you know when something is clear and briefly tell you why. If something is not clear, it should be kindly indicated with "I am not sure what you are saying here. Perhaps a different word choice would help." Even if the feedback is not as clear, learn to recognize the intent of your reviewer (or ask questions!). Then take that advice as constructive and work towards a resolution.
- **Be kind**. Above all else, kindness goes a long way. Many seemingly discouraging criticisms have been delivered in a kind way and been received as encouraging. As long as the message is constructive in nature and positive in tone you should feel free to take it into consideration.
- **The process is different from the presentation**. What this means is that even though the end result of a writing project should be conversational, the process of building that conversation is quite different from the presentation. Academic conversations are not spontaneous. They take research, thought, patience and a keen understanding of your main idea and your audience. Be aware of this process in your own writing, and whether you have received specific feedback in certain areas from your reviewer or not, look for those areas that depend on clarity of research, thought, patience, understanding, relatability and review.

Integrating Sources

Integrating your sources is an important part of the writing process, because we writers are borrowing from the research and expertise of others to assist in developing our own claims. It is important to provide proper credit when we borrow tis information. We often engage in direct quotation because there is something critical about the precise phrasing of the source; other times, we will paraphrase by putting someone else's ideas or concepts into our own words. Paraphrases tend to be roughly same in length as the original material and represent an important skill in academic writing. Regardless of whether you quote or paraphrase, **you must provide credit**. In MLA citation format, this means that you provide the author's last name and the page number from the original source where the information came from. In APA format, you will also include the year the source was published. For details on MLA and APA citation formats, we recommend consulting the OWL @ Purdue, an open-access online resource.

There are many ways to integrate sources with skill and variety. Below, we draw upon a worksheet first created at Saint Joseph College's Center for Academic Excellence. Many instructors have found this a helpful and practical guide for integrating sources with skill and variation—a simple and effective way to "step up" your academic writing in a way that will be recognized by your instructor.

The examples below utilize introductory phrases to signal to beginning of a quotation. This is a skillful approach because it integrates the quotation directly into the context of the writer's own sentence. Because the quoted author's name is mentioned in the introductory phrase, there is no need to include the last name in the parenthetical citation. Note, as well, that the quotation closes before the parenthetical citation and that the period **follows** the close of the citation. It is a common error to place the period before the parenthetical citation; getting it right evidences attention to detail in a way your instructor is likely to notice.

Below, you will see the same quotation being integrated in increasingly skilled ways. We recommend that you become skilled at using key words and ellipsis style quotations whenever appropriate, for this evidences strong ability ad reveal that you are most interested in using only the most appropriate words and phrases from a quote, rather than filling up your essay with long quotations to help achieve word length requirements. After these quotes, you will see many verbs that can be used to provide clarity and variation to your quotations. We recommend practicing many techniques with many kinds of signal verbs.

Whole quotation

Samuel Johnson claims that "Shakespeare is, above all other writers, at least above all modern writers, the poet of nature, the poet that holds up to his readers a faithful mirror of manners and of life" (301).

Part of a quotation

Samuel Johnson contends that Shakespeare's writing is superior to other poets' because he was "the poet of nature, the poet that holds up to his readers a faithful mirror of manners and of life" (301).

Key words

Samuel Johnson praises Shakespeare for being "the poet of nature," believing that he surpassed all other poets in his ability to construct "a faithful mirror of manners and of life" (301).

Note: When two quotations in a sentence come from the same page, the page number appears only after the second quotation.

Ellipses (…)

Johnson claims that "Shakespeare is, above all other writers…the poet of nature, the poet that holds up to his readers a faithful mirror of manners and of life" (301).

A Selection of Verbs to Use in Signal Phrases

Acknowledges	Claims	Discloses	Implies	Recounts	Submits
Adds	Comments	Discounts	Indicates	Refers	Suggests
Admits	Compares	Disputes	Insists	Reflects	Supports
Advances	Concludes	Documents	Maintains	Refutes	Theorizes
Affirms	Concurs	Emphasize	Narrates	Reiterates	Writes
Agrees	Confirms	Explains	Negates	Relates	Verifies
Alludes	Contends	Expresses	Notes	Remarks	
Argues	Contrasts	Extrapolates	Observes	Replies	
Asserts	Declares	Grants	Points our	Reports	
Attests	Defines	Highlights	Posits	Responds	
Characterizes	Delineates	Hypothesizes	Purports	Reveals	
Chronicles	Denies	Illustrates	Reasons	States	

Keep in mind that sources are mostly needed where they will add the most clarity and support to OUR argument. Sources are like close friends. They do not speak for us, but they always "have our back".

For example, in Nicole Gonzalez's essay entitled "What It Means to Represent Transgender Identities on Television," Gonzalez takes a common approach and utilizes paraphrase when he writes that "54% of the 102 episodes that included transgender characters on TV were categorized as containing negative depictions" and a direct quote when he states that "'anti-transgender slurs, language and dialogue was presented in at least 61% of the cataloged episodes and storylines'" from "GLAAD's 2002 television report" to add weight to her claim that "transgender identities are still being underrepresented" (28[1]). When you visit the article in your copy of *Comp@Central* in the back of this book, notice how neither use of her source speaks *for* Gonzalez.

> ### Exercise
>
> Take a moment or two to analyze how well your sources "have your back". On a separate piece of paper or on a printed draft, highlight the sentence before your paraphrase or quote - does this sentence lead into or set up the source material to come? If not, then your source is speaking for you. You are strong, you are confident, you are a practicing college writer, how can you add or revise the sentence that comes before your source material to include your claim and how your source speaks to it?

[1] © Nicole Gonzalez

CHAPTER 4

Writing Craft

by Rebecca Arruda and Moriah Maresh

Introduction

In this chapter we are inviting you to think about writing as something that needs to be *crafted*. Like other crafts such as woodworking, songwriting, and sculpting, it takes practice to become skillful and proficient. And it means that writing is a process—not just for you, but for all writers.

One of the things you'll be working on this semester is developing an academic voice and style that uniquely belongs to you. When we talk about a writer's voice, we are talking about the way they look at the world through their unique lens and how they communicate that. Just like every person has a unique speaking voice, we all have unique writing voices. But unlike our speaking voices, we can develop our writing voices so they "sound" the way we want to readers. We can learn to control our written voice much more than our spoken voice. That's important because voice helps establish our ethos for readers. It gives them a sense of who we are, how we think about our topic, and how we feel about it.

While we don't have a spoken voice in our writing, readers will "hear" a voice in their heads as they read any piece of writing. Some essays or articles just "sound" different than others. And we are going to work on honing and using that. You may be wondering *how* a writer could possibly control something like voice. *Don't we just write how we write?* Well, no, actually. In this chapter, we'll discuss writing style, which refers to the words we choose and the order we put our sentences in. Style helps establish our voice, and the more we learn about writing style, the more tools we have to control our voice.

To summarize: Voice is how you sound or come across to your audience. It is the lens through which you write (values, interests, preferences, beliefs). Style is the way the words are captured on the page through word choice and sentence structure.

Style and voice are closely related. We use style in order to establish our voice. With voice and style so intimately connected, you may ask how do we intertwine them together and still recognize them as their own entities? Read on to find out!

Voice

How you craft your voice when you sit down to write depends on many factors. Spoiler alert: these factors are rhetorical. Stop and think about this. Your voice is uniquely yours, but it is impacted by your purpose (what you are trying to achieve), your audience (who you want to persuade/your target readers), your context (events taking place that motivate you to write), and your genre (the recognizable form you are writing in, such as an essay or a tweet). If you are writing on social media, perhaps you are establishing yourself as having valid and strong opinions and are worth listening to. Maybe you've discovered a niche market and are constructing your own channel to reach as many viewers as possible. Finding your voice in a classroom at Central could mean you are working on building your self-confidence by increasing your participation level and realizing what you say is important. When you find your voice on a sports team, you are most likely taking on a leadership role and aiding your team in working together to form bonds and develop common goals.

In college writing, we want to establish our academic voice, which uses more formal language and avoids the everyday speech we use when talking or texting with friends. By keeping your audience in mind (your professors and your peers) you will craft your academic voice and cultivate a clear style.

Finding Your Academic Voice

At this stage in your composition class, you may not know what your academic voice sounds like at all—and that's okay. College writing is a discovery process that includes learning more about your perspective as a student and a person. And as you are discovering your perspective, you'll also be learning to think rhetorically and make choices about your writing style (the words and sentence structure you use).

Try the following exercise to begin understanding how your voice sounds to you and to others.

Exercise

Read over a paragraph you've written in the past (one from a college class if you can) and list five adjectives to describe yourself as a writer. Now give the same paragraph to a friend and ask them to list five adjectives that describe you as a writer. Are there any words that match exactly or are close? What patterns emerge when you look at these adjectives?

Your adjectives (about yourself)	Your friend's adjectives (about you)
1. _____	1. _____
2. _____	2. _____
3. _____	3. _____
4. _____	4. _____
5. _____	5. _____

Another concept that is useful when we're thinking about our voice and style is tone. In writing, tone is your attitude about a particular topic. Tone, like voice, gets communicated through your word choice. You can use either a formal or an informal tone, depending on the assignment you are writing. For example, a narrative essay will be about a personal story, so naturally the writing would be more informal or casual. In contrast, a researched argument essay is about you joining an existing conversation on a particular subject alongside experts in their field. Your tone will sound more formal to enhance your credibility.

Exercise

Read the following sentences and decide whether you think the tone sounds formal or informal. Then determine what the overall tone is by choosing adjectives that describe the feeling/mood the sentence projects.

1. Although the star-filled sky was gorgeous, her mood was so melancholic that she took no interest in it.
2. The presentation of the sunrise was so astounding that people stood watching breathlessly.
3. The negotiations between the two countries came to a halt after the terms of reference could not be agreed upon.
4. They went into the diner and ordered a hot coffee, and the cozy atmosphere inside reminded them of the past.

Voice and Genre Expectations

In the chapter on genre, we define it as "A particular style or category of works of art; especially a type of literary work characterized by a particular form, style, or purpose" (oed.com). You may have noticed by now that *all* concepts in writing are linked, and this includes genre expectations and voice. Once you have decided on a particular genre you will be writing in, it's time to add your own voice and style, always keeping the audience's expectations in mind. If you are writing a rhetorical analysis, for example, you'll want to use an academic voice that is clear and confident, showcasing your credibility. Your voice will be conveyed through your individual word choices as you analyze another writer's text. You'll aim for word choice that sounds like you, but a formal version of yourself.

Let's look at an example from a student essay to understand genre, voice, and tone a bit more.

The following is an excerpt from a rhetorical analysis essay titled, "Rhetorical Analysis of Kenneth Goldsmith," by Maslin Laberge. As you read the paragraph below, take notes on the word choice. What words stand out to you? Is the language formal or informal? What is your impression of the writer?

"It's likely that when Homo Habilis sharpened the first stick into a spear, one of his fellow cavemen complained about the good old days when clubs were all they needed. In the countless millennia since, human technology progressed considerably, always with similar debates about its use" (Laberge 11[1]).

Writing Style

In the first half of this chapter, we explored the idea of voice. In essence, your writing voice is the lens through which you view the world. Your voice is you, your personality, your outlook. On the page, voice can be influenced by your writing tone, which offers a more specific attitude about your subject. Both your voice and tone can be influenced by our next focus: style. While your voice is the lens through which you experience the world, your style is how you express that experience. Style consists of how you manipulate words on the page. Think of your style as piecing together legos. If everyone in your class were given the same amount of legos and told to build something, every structure would be different! When you write, build, craft, and create. Let's consider an example of two different writing styles. First, read the beginning of William Golding's *Lord of the Flies*, in which we are introduced to Ralph, the protagonist:

> The boy with fair hair lowered himself down the last few feet of rock and began to pick his way toward the lagoon. Though he had taken off his school sweater and trailed it now from one hand, his grey shirt stuck to him and his hair was plastered to his forehead.

Now, let's change it up by varying sentence length, structure, placement of information, and word choice:

> The boy lowered himself down the last few feet of rock. His light-colored hair stuck to his forehead, and his grey shirt clung to his skin, even though he had taken off his school sweater. He dragged it behind him with one hand as he made his way toward the lagoon.

---

[1] © Maslin Laberge

These two examples provide information about Ralph's situation but sound different. What are some of the key differences you observe?

_____

_____

_____

_____

How do the sentences vary? Were any sentences combined or split up? What words were changed? Discuss how these changes affected your impression of the passages. How did you interpret the writer's attitude? How did each passage make you feel?

Let's think in greater detail about aspects that influence style, such as word choice, sentence structure, and grammar.

Word Choice

Have you ever re-read a text or an email before clicking "send"? Have you ever made a statement or asked a question and then wished you had worded your thoughts differently? Have you ever thought, "Wow!" after listening to a speech? These are examples of the influence of word choice. The various sounds and implications of words can affect an audience, and learning to harness this ability can increase your credibility and impact. Let's look at this example:

> The vocabulary you use in your writing impacts your readers' impressions of you and the information you present.

> The lexicon employed in your writing influences your audience's perception of you as well as your topic.

These two sentences mean relatively the same thing but have different effects. The first example is more laid-back, yet straightforward. The second example uses more advanced vocabulary. When writing for an academic audience, more advanced language can increase your ethos. Let's explore another example:

> Social media can cause a lot of harm because people can bully and be mean online since they can hide behind a screen.

> Social media can be harmful due to cyberbullying and people using fake profiles to spread hate speech without direct consequences.

Again, these examples are quite similar in meaning, but they use different styles. Which one do you think sounds more academic? Why?

_____

_____

_____

Besides increasing your credibility, word choice can impact your reader's overall reading experience by evoking emotions and imagination. Let's return to our _Lord of the Flies_ example, this time paying attention to the underlined words:

> The boy with <u>fair</u> hair lowered himself down the last few feet of rock and began <u>to pick his way</u> toward the lagoon. Though he had taken off his school sweater and <u>trailed</u> it now from one hand, his grey shirt <u>stuck</u> to him and his hair was <u>plastered</u> to his forehead.

The boy lowered himself down the last few feet of rock. His <u>light-colored</u> hair stuck to his forehead, and his grey shirt <u>clung</u> to his skin, even though he had taken off his school sweater. He <u>dragged</u> it behind him with one hand as he <u>made his way</u> toward the lagoon.

What are the effects of the different word choices?

fair vs. light-colored

_____

to pick his way vs. made his way

_____

trailed vs. dragged

_____

stuck vs. clung

_____

plastered vs. stuck

_____

In these examples, neither word choice is right nor wrong. They just encourage different images. However, there are times when word choice can be right or wrong. Let's take an example from a hypothetical student, Julia:

Social media can cause some harm. People can be mean online since they can hide behind a screen. Cyberbullying needs to stop.

Based on these sentences, what do we think of Julia's voice (lens through which she views the world)? Does she think social media is a little dangerous? Very dangerous? Does she think bullying is a serious problem online? When asked these questions by her instructor, Julia expresses that she thinks social media is extremely dangerous and provides concrete examples of how people were negatively affected by cyberbullies. This response is quite different than what she expressed in her writing. The instructor offers this feedback:

You write "some harm"—does that mean you believe it is not a lot of harm?
"Can" is used three times in two sentences, and reads to me like "might." Is that what you think?
Could you include examples? You say cyberbullying needs to stop, but why? Think about your audience. Remember the rhetorical situation. Maybe your readers have never been cyberbullied, and you want to help those readers understand.

Considering this feedback and your own ideas, how could Julia change her writing style to express her perspective?

_____

_____

_____

Julia considers her instructor's advice. She adjusts some vocabulary and elaborates on her thoughts:

I think social media causes a lot of harm to people who use it. People hide behind their screens and bully others anonymously about personal stuff. There are a lot of people who have become anxious, depressed, and even suicidal due to cyberbullying. Needless to say, social media can be a very dangerous tool that needs to be monitored closely.

How has Julia improved her argument?

_____

_____

_____

Again, Julia gets feedback from her instructor:

Much better!—great job revising. You are providing more insight and strengthening your argument. However, I'd like you to state your point more clearly and strongly. Remember that your reader knows you are the one writing, so whatever you write is what you think. Be aware of <u>filler words </u>and <u>lazy language</u>.

In this example, Julia's instructor asks her to make her point more clearly. Doing so will involve cutting some words she calls "filler" and "lazy" to help make her writing more concise. Keep reading to find out what we mean by "filler words" and "lazy language."

Some filler words:

Filler words and lazy language are extra words that detract from your argument. Filler words are sometimes called "fluff." Some writers think that these unneeded words make their writing sound more academic and credible when, in reality, they waste page space.

Whether or not a word can be called "filler" or "lazy" depends on how you use it, but there are some common words to watch for in your writing because they are often unnecessary. As you read through your own writing, ask yourself whether a word really adds meaning and consider what would happen if you cut it.

Here are some examples:

that

Most of the time, "that" is unnecessary. Review any time you use "that" in your paper. If you remove it from the sentence, does it still make sense?

"I think that we should get coffee."
vs.
"I think we should get coffee."

Keep in mind: "That" also serves as an article (this vs. that). In these cases, "that" is required to differentiate one thing from another.

needless to say

If your point is truly needless, then why would you say it?

"Needless to say, we had a great time at the beach."
vs.
"We had a great time at the beach."

just

"Just" is often used when we don't want to sound rude or we want to lessen the impact of what we say. But in academic writing, you want to own your position. In most cases, adding "just" isn't necessary. You have our permission to make your point clearly and boldly.

> "I just think social media is a beneficial tool."
> vs.
> "I think social media is a beneficial tool."

in my opinion

Your reader is already reading your paper, so they know the content is your opinion! Drawing attention to your opinion doesn't add much.

> "In my opinion, we should all try to recycle more."
> vs.
> "We should all try to recycle more."

Some lazy language:

Lazy language consists of words that are unclear or too broad. For instance, if a friend said he is going to the store to get "stuff," do you know what he is actually getting? Or, what if he said he did some fun "things" last weekend. What does that mean? Lazy language can always either be omitted or replaced by more specific words. Consider these examples:

stuff / things

"Stuff" and "things" are two of the laziest words out there! 99% of the time, they can be replaced by more specific nouns.

> "A lot of the stuff he posts online is intense."
> vs.
> "A lot of the content he posts online is intense."

> "There are a lot of things in that store."
> vs.
> "There are a lot of products in that store."

very/really

These words can often be replaced by more specific adjectives.

> "I was really happy you came to my party."
> vs.
> "I was grateful you came to my party. Seeing you made me extremely happy."

This second option provides the reader with more insight. If you see "really" or "very" in your writing, consider a more specific adjective that could express your point.

went

"Went" can often be replaced by a more specific verb.

> "We went to the store."
> vs.
> "We drove to the store."

small/big

While there is nothing wrong with simpler adjectives like "small" and "big," part of developing your style is your specificity.

"The doll is small."
vs.
"The doll is miniature."

"That house is big."
vs.
"That house is massive."

Considering what we have learned about filler words and lazy language, let's return to Julia's argument:

I think social media causes a lot of harm to people who use it. People hide behind their screens and bully others anonymously about personal stuff. There are a lot of people who have become anxious, depressed, and even suicidal due to cyberbullying. Needless to say, social media can be a very dangerous tool that needs to be monitored very closely.

How might Julia edit her work to omit filler words and lazy language?

_____

_____

_____

_____

_____

Sentence Structure

Let's return to our comparison from earlier in the chapter: writing style is like a lego tower. If word choice is the blocks, then sentence structure is how you arrange those blocks. That arrangement can result in dramatically different outcomes! In order to discuss sentence structure, we first need a basic understanding of the parts of a sentence. While we aren't doing a deep dive into grammar instruction here, we want to establish some basics about sentence structure so you can be a more informed and thorough editor of your own writing.

The simplest sentences are made of two parts:

subject + verb

Subject = who/what the sentence is about; who/what performs the action
Verb = the action
Ex: I ran. Collin played. The butterfly flew.
Though brief, these sentences present complete thoughts. Someone is running, and that someone is mentioned. Someone is playing, and we learn that someone is Collin. A bug is flying, and that bug is a butterfly. However, most sentences, especially in academic writing, consist of at least

three parts (and often, multiple clauses and phrases are connected to form complex sentence structures). A sentence with three parts includes:

subject + verb + object

Subject = who/what the sentence is about; who/what performs the action
Verb = the action
Object = who/what is acted upon
Ex: The man painted the house. Stella returned the library book. The students submitted their homework.
What did the man paint? The house. What did Stella return? The library book. What did the students submit? Their homework.

A common error is when a writer leaves out the subject. Even if you mention the subject in a previous sentence, *who* or *what* is taking the action needs to be present in every sentence.

Ex: A lot of people enjoy skiing. Going cross-country skiing or downhill.
Who/what is going cross-country or downhill? There are several ways we can add a subject to this sentence.

Option 1: Add the subject.
A lot of people enjoy skiing. Skiers go cross-country skiing or downhill.

Option 2: Combine the sentences.
A lot of people enjoy skiing, whether cross-country skiing or downhill.
In order to combine the complete sentence with the incomplete sentence without a subject, we added a comma and a conjunction, or connecting word (in this case, "whether").

This is only the basics of sentence structure. For more information on sentence structure you can explore the resources from the Writing Center or the online resource, Purdue Owl.

Conclusion

Voice and style take time to develop. A helpful way to recognize your voice and how it is impacted by your style is to read your writing aloud, record yourself reading, or have someone read your work to you. By hearing what has been written, writers tend to have an easier time recognizing their strengths ("My introduction sounds intelligent and passionate!") and areas that need improvement ("That complicated vocabulary actually sounds distracting."). Remember: Voice and style are not developed overnight. Just as our physical voices have evolved and matured over the course of our lives, so do our writing voices. The more in tune you become with your current voice and style, the easier (and more fun!) it will be to explore and manipulate how you present yourself and your ideas on the page.

CHAPTER 5

Engaging with Sources

by Jessyka Scoppetta

Your instructor just introduced your next writing assignment and part of the requirements include using 3–5 scholarly sources. You might be thinking, what does that mean? What is a scholarly source? Where do I find one? How do I make sure I am choosing good sources and finding the best information I can? How can I put this information in my paper? These are all excellent questions!

At some point in your academic career, you will be assigned a research paper. In a first year WRT course, you will almost certainly do research which will require you to engage with sources. Perhaps you got to pick a topic or maybe one has been selected for you. You might be starting with a question, a working thesis, or crafting an argument in order to join an existing academic conversation. Whatever the content of your writing assignment, you need sources to help you better understand your topic and expand your ideas. This chapter will be your guide as you select, evaluate, and integrate sources, and engage in the research process.

Finding Useful and Credible Sources

Whether your purpose is to inform or persuade, the quality of your sources will enhance your own credibility with your audience. So choose wisely! Aim to select sources that are objective, accurate, and appropriate for your topic.

Consider Research as a Process (or Research as Exploration)

One important thing to keep in mind even before you start looking for sources is that research is a process, much like writing is a process. To be successful, you must be willing to engage in the research process and let yourself explore. Searching for sources might take some time. You might have to hone and revise your research question or key search terms. You might have to try multiple databases and online searches. You may find sources that steer you down a path you didn't expect. Or you might wander around and find yourself at a dead end. This is all perfectly normal. The higher your tolerance for exploration in your research process, the more likely you are to find the best sources to make your argument. All that said, there is a balance between exploration and not being able to see the forest through the trees. Maintaining focus, even as you wander, is key.

Choosing Your Sources

Research writing gives you the opportunity to engage with a variety of sources—books, scholarly journals, films, reports, newspaper articles—just to name a few. To determine what kind of sources will be the most effective, you will want to consider your audience and your purpose for writing. Many times, your instructor will help set up audience expectations by requiring a certain type of source. But that is not always the case, and you will first need to determine which kinds of sources would be most appropriate for your research assignment.

Understanding more about various types of sources can help you make smart choices. One-way sources can be categorized as either **primary** or **secondary** sources.

Primary sources are the original documents, artifacts, or research or first-hand accounts of information.

Examples of primary sources include interviews; art; performances; speeches; diaries; letters; original documents; research studies that present new findings; data sets; census records; case law; legislation; and unedited photographs, video, or audio that capture an event.

Secondary sources aim to summarize, describe, analyze, evaluate, and/or provide commentary on primary sources, and thus are at least one step removed for the original document, data, or event. Secondary sources often seek to better understand the information presented in the primary sources involved.

Examples of secondary sources include textbooks; reference books like encyclopedias; newspaper op-eds; some scholarly sources like journal articles that analyze existing research; books; criticism of art and literature; histories; and documentaries.

Exercise

Each year, the President of the United States gives a State of the Union Address to Congress and the American public. Google the latest State of the Union Address and review the first page or two of sources. What kinds of sources are you finding (videos, new articles, press releases, etc.)? What do these sources look like? What are they saying? What do you think their purpose is? How would you categorize these sources: primary or secondary sources? If you are looking to draw your own conclusions about what was said at the State of Union, which of these sources would be most appropriate and why?

Definition

According to the Library of Congress, "Primary sources are the raw materials of history—original documents and objects which were created at the time under study. They are different from secondary sources, accounts, or interpretations of events created by someone without firsthand experience" (https://www.loc.gov/programs/teachers/getting-started-with-primary-sources/).

Journal articles are a main source of information for scholars, researchers, and students. Generally, these articles will fall into one of two categories: **popular** or **scholarly** sources. As mentioned before, many professors will require you to search for peer-reviewed, or scholarly sources. Peer-reviewed or scholarly sources tend to be favored in the academic world because the information they present is more detailed and they have been more thoroughly vetted than popular sources. But just because scholarly sources are often privileged by academia does not mean that popular sources are not appropriate in certain circumstances. If you need general information about a topic or if you have a topic that focuses on current events, then popular sources will probably be more useful to you. Here's a chart that further explains the differences between popular sources and scholarly sources:

	POPULAR	SCHOLARLY
Length	Short articles	Lengthy, in-depth articles
Purpose	To inform readers of topics; present a broad overview of a topic; entertain	Communicate research findings; present new developments in a field of study; education
Audience	General readership without a particular background, expertise, or advanced education; Vocabulary appropriate for a general audience and concepts are summarized to be easy to understand	Intended for specialist readership of researchers, academics, students, and professionals uses technical, subject-specific language and jargon
Author	Written by publication staff, journalists, bloggers, or generalists. Sometimes no author is listed.	Written by scientists, researchers, historians, and specialists in a particular subject area
Design	Designed to attract an audience; may include a catchy title, photographs or illustrations, and be paired with advertisements	Stark, professional design. Mostly text, unless presenting data in charts and graphs. No advertisements. They follow a discipline-specific format, which usually includes an abstract, introduction, literature review, methodology, conclusion, and list of references
Editorial Process	Edited and approved for publication in-house, not peer-reviewed	Peer reviewed, meaning it was critically evaluated by peers in the field for content, relevance, and academic value
Documentation	May link to sources or mention them in the text, but no formal citations or list of references.	Contains in-text citations or footnotes and a list of references at the end. Will follow the documentation style of its discipline.
Examples	*The New York Times, Time Magazine, Vogue, Newsweek*	*College Composition and Communication, Psychological Review, The Journal of Experimental Biology*

Internet Resources

How to Search the Web

While many of us are comfortable with popular search engines such as **Google** and **Bing** and how they work, many of us still may struggle with how to get the best results. To begin, navigate to the search page of your chosen search engine and type in the search term or terms relative to the topic you would like to begin researching. Keep it simple and direct at first.

For this example, we are exploring the topic of *role-playing*. Here are some of the initial results of preliminary research:

Notice that the first entry that is listed is a definition of your search terms—don't blow by it! Take this arrangement into account as knowing a definition of what you are researching is key to beginning to understand your topic. This is why it comes first in your internet search! In turn, passing a definition of your search term along to your audience should be a key element early on in *your* conversation. After you have read the definition and considered the meaning, you can scroll down further for more comprehensive results.

As our intent is to explore role-playing through video games, choosing to click on a listing that includes "game" in the description is a good first choice to start. In this case, the first in the list is from Wikipedia.

Wikipedia has undergone many improvements since its launch in 2000. At first, entries were generally uncited, lacked scholarly insight, and could be edited by anyone with a computer keyboard, so the use of Wikipedia in an academic discussion was widely discouraged. Today, while Wikipedia remains an unreliable primary or secondary source—unless your discussion is on Wikipedia itself, it is a good resource for quick information to get you started. Another resource that should be approached with caution are News sites.

News sites have gone through their own transformation over the recent few years. All have come from the point of view of popular culture, but in recent years much of the information that comes to us through news sites has become increasingly polarized. What we need to look for now are news sources that have a consistent reputation for reporting impartially or without prejudice. In other words, a news source that reports the facts with little to no influence from opinion.

A good place to start is with news sources that are non-profit and/or publicly funded such as The Associated Press and NPR. While both have been described as "left-leaning," sources such as C-SPAN have a solid reputation for fact checking while the BBC is known for its impartiality. Other sources like USA-Today are known for including many viewpoints on the same topic as a way of representing impartiality as a news source. During the 1960's through the 1980's, the landscape of reputable news outlets changed dramatically when news outlets came under the direction of large conglomerates and began to rely more on ratings than public service. During this time, the CBS Evening News generated the best reputation for reliable news and anchor Walter Cronkite became the "most trusted man in America." Today, the key to finding a good news source is to find one that is not full of dramatic effect or trying to convince you of something good or bad, but one that is simply reporting the facts.

Exercise

Go to YouTube and look for a video of Walter Cronkite on the CBS Evening News. Watch the full video, with commercials (because the commercials are the best part!). Begin to notice how Cronkite acts and reacts to what he is reporting. Then consider the reporting itself by choosing one segment. How does Cronkite describe the situation? What words does he use in describing the situation? Does he attempt to influence his audience one way or the other in how they should feel about a situation? If so, using what words? Then watch one or two more. Does Cronkite's mood change? Do his words change to add more dramatic effect?

In the United States of America, a **.gov** site belongs to an official government organization. We are most familiar with IRS.gov or USA.gov, which are credible resources and can lead you to more than 6000 other credible government sites. The one area of concern is political websites whose intent is to influence public opinion. Here again, if you are presented with more than just the facts—if someone is trying to convince you of something—then opinion is a work and you should proceed with caution.

After we have looked into the basics of our main topic and gathered some preliminary information and resources for our research, now we can get down to the specifics of purpose. **Google Scholar** is a search engine similar to Google, which takes that same simple, broad view, but applies it to scholarly literature. If we expand on our search terms and include our basic purpose, role-playing in video games, we can begin to find scholarly sources to help back the author's claims.

Here, we will find many scholarly articles on role-playing in video games and can choose our intent, which means the intention or purpose of building this academic conversation. In other words, why are we exploring role-playing in video games? If our purpose is to claim that video games offer more societal benefits than detractions, then we can be more focused with our search terms.

In focusing his search terms, we can provide more specific and varied insight into how playing video games does not necessarily lead to aggressive behavior. With the ideas of opinion and potential aggressive behavior in mind, the use of social media as a source can be a tricky one.

In utilizing **Social Media** for a scholarly topic for research, you should first consider the "social" of social media. Google tells us that *social* is "relating to society or its organization" and "an informal social gathering, especially one organized by the members of a particular club or group." In the case of scholarly work, we need to look for those resources that are more formal than informal and have less to do with a specific club or group. Take **YouTube**. The key to using social media sources such as YouTube is awareness of what you are viewing. What you are watching may use facts, but does it represent only the perspective of one group?

Another reliable and valuable resource for learning on social media is through **Image, Video and/or Audio Repositories** such as TED Conferences, LLC. More commonly referred to as **TED Talks**, discussions are produced on various and varying topics, collected, stored and can be accessed at no cost to the consumer. What is most helpful to early college writers and researchers is TED-Ed. Here is a transcript of a Podcast found by searching "video games cause aggression."

Your instructors may have further suggestions on what reliable social media platforms will work best for you depending on the focus of your work within each writing class.

The form of Social Media that may be best utilized for education is for student communication. Zoom, WebEx, and Teams are all good meeting platforms for student study groups or general class meetings when the weather or some other public concern disrupts our ability to be together in person.

Unlike Facebook and Instagram, which are public platforms, Blackboard, Canvas, and other learning platforms are great for recording and storing grades, discussions, commentary, and email communications within a focused group. Because of this, they are private and not accessible or editable by everyone. While nothing replaces the depth of conversation had in an in-person group gathering, the next best thing is a closed social media space where participants feel kindly encouraged and supported.

Evaluating Sources

Once you find sources, you will want to consider their usefulness to your project. Sometimes a source might seem like a winner because it uses your search terms or has a compelling title and abstract, but ultimately it doesn't help you with your purpose for writing. Or perhaps on second glance, you don't think it will be persuasive to your audience. Keeping audience and purpose in mind can help you make determinations about whether or not to use a source. You will also want to determine whether or not your source is a credible source of information and appropriate for a college-level paper. Here are some questions to ask to help you analyze your potential sources:

1. **What is the source's main claim or idea?** Does this idea make sense to you? Have you seen similar ideas in your reading and research? Is this idea supported by evidence?

2. **What is the genre?** Is this a news report? A research study? An op-ed? Depending on your purpose and audience, you might only be looking for sources that report information, like a research study or government report. In other cases, you may be looking for opinion pieces that offer a variety of perspectives on a topic.

3. **Who is the author(s)?** What are their credentials and background? Who are they affiliated with? What is their purpose in writing? If you can't find out more about an author on the source, you can use Google to find out more information on any author. Some will have that information on their webpage in an "About Us" section.

4. **Who is the publisher or organization?** Who is putting out this information about why? As with authors, you can use Google to find out more information on any publisher or organization. Do they have a bias or agenda you should be aware of? What is their purpose? Many will have that information on their webpage in an "About Us" section. If it's an online source, the URL can give you clues who is sponsoring the website: .org is used by nonprofits; .gov are government agencies; .com is for commerce; and .edu is for colleges and universities. URLS don't automatically make a source credible or not, but they are tools to help you determine what is appropriate for your paper.

5. **When was it published?** Depending on your topic, timeliness matters. If you are writing about Victorian Literature, when your sources were published probably does not matter. But a topic like best practices in nursing would privilege sources published within the last 5–10 years. If you are writing on current events, then perhaps your sources would need to be no more than a few weeks or months old.

6. **Does it contain links to supporting sources and/or cite sources?** Scholarly sources should always include a list of references and some type of in-text citations. But reputable popular sources will also offer information about sources, just in a more informal way. It is very important if you are using a secondary source, that your source gives you the information you need to link back to the primary sources. In order to trust what is written, you need to know where that information comes from.

7. **What bias may be present or does the source seem objective?** Every media source is biased in some way. You can't get away from that. But you should look for sources that strive for objectivity. There are some news publications that are very well respected and are considered objective, despite some liberal or conservative bias: *The Wall Street Journal, The New York Times, The Washington Post, The BBC, NPR, The Atlantic, The Economist, The New Yorker, Politico.* Also, consider that a source that addresses criticism, identifies bias, or details other ways of thinking in some way generally is more credible as well.

8. **Ultimately, do you think you can trust the information in this article, and do you feel confident using it in a college-level assignment? Why or why not?** Or in other words, is it appropriate for academic work? Why or why not? The sources you choose to include in your assignment build your ethos as a writer. Make sure you can stand behind the sources that you cite.

Recognizing Fake News

Because there are more ways than ever today that people get their news, the amount of information out there has increased tremendously. Unfortunately, not all that information is accurate. In fact, some of it is intentionally misleading or false. Therefore, as consumers of news, we have to be even more vigilant about the news we choose to read, share, and use. The chart below offers a blueprint for how to critically examine a source to determine whether or not it is fake.

Fact Checking Tools

There are also useful websites dedicated to helping people determine whether or not news is factual. These three organizations can help you determine whether or not the information presented in your sources is credible and trustworthy: Snopes.com, Factcheck.org, PolitiFact.com.

How to Spot Fake News

To spot fake news and/or identify unreliable sources, consider the following approaches.

First, think about the source. Is it reliable? Check the website, including mission and other editorial statements.

Second, Google the author. What can you learn about this person's experiences or bias that could be problematic?

Third, how recent is the source?

Fourth, read deeply into an article to be sure you understand it correctly.

Fifth, does the source provide its own supporting sources to "back" up its claims?

Sixth, make sure you are not accidentally reading a satirical website like The Onion or Reductress. These websites imitate legitimate sources for comedic effect.

Seventh, you should consult with CCSU librarians and other qualified experts who can help you figure out if what you are reading is reliable.

And finally—always check your own biases as they may blind you to legitimate sources that express points of view challenging your own.

Figure 5.1 How to spot fake news.

Exercise

Remember that much of what we read on social media is superficial at best. Be part of the solution, not part of the problem—check your bias at the door. It's fine to have opinions, just remember to form those opinions based on solid facts rather than what you think you remember. Influencers rely on your willingness to be satisfied with just keywords and dramatic effect. Keep in mind that you don't want to become a wishful thinker when it comes to research, you want to be aware of the details, good, bad or indifferent. For this exercise, you will become the influencer and root out your own bias. This exercise can be done in a group (one person taking on the role of announcer) or on your own. In completing this exercise, you will see how these influencers operate:

1. What article have you chosen to share with us today?
2. Have you used inflammatory language in your tagline? What words are you using to cause dramatic effect?
3. Have you included a parody of actual events to entertain and to draw your audience in? What does it include?
4. Are you speaking to your reader from a particular point of view? Are you trying to influence them, how? What are some of the words that you use as influencers?
5. Are you using sensationalized, misleading or exaggerated words or images that are unrelated to your news to draw readers in? What are they?
6. Are you using graphics or word choice to mimic a particular type of reputable source as a cloaking device? Who are you mimicking and why?
7. When a reader clicks on your story, are they flooded with links to other stories or advertisements? What stories/advertisements are they and how do they relate?
8. When a reader clicks on your story, do you do nothing more than repeat the same message over and over without ever developing it? What message do you repeat?

Annotated Bibliography

A common exercise that writers engage with during a research assignment is an annotated bibliography (this topic is also discussed in the chapter Writing Processes). An annotated bibliography consists of a list of citations of the sources you are considering using for your paper. Each citation is then followed by a summary of that source and brief commentary about the usefulness or relevance of that source to your research project.

Annotated bibliographies have several purposes. First, it can help you organize the materials you have collected during your research. Second, compiling the annotated bibliography forces you to read your sources more carefully and begin to evaluate their relevance to your research project. Third, the annotated bibliography may also help you to see patterns, themes, or gaps you have in your research and help you narrow your focus or determine where you might need to search further. Finally, it gives you a list of citations and summaries at your fingertips for when you are ready to start writing your research paper.

A Quick Guide to Annotated Bibliography:

1. Choose your documentation style, if it has not been provided by your professor. This will determine how your citations look.
2. Identify the author and the type of source.
3. Briefly summarize the source's main points.
4. Discuss how the source contributes to your research or helps inform you about your topic.
5. Alphabetize your entries by the lead author's name. If there is no author, use the lead word of the title.

    Make sure your format is accurate and consistent.

Integrating Sources With Integrity and Intention

In the academic world, ideas are of the utmost value because the research, theories, and analyses you put forth are how you contribute to your community, your field of study, and to the world. Therefore, crediting others' words and ideas is incredibly important. Ideas are meant to be shared and discussed, but you have to give credit to the source.

As a student, the responsibility you have is two-fold: First, any work that you turn in at CCSU needs to be your work. It can't come from a friend, a sibling, or the Internet. Second, if your work draws on information from others, you need to properly cite both their words and their ideas. Readers should understand which ideas and words are yours and which came from sources.

Once you have found the sources you need, your next step is to put those sources in conversation with your ideas in ways that advance your argument. The sources you bring together should help you achieve your writing purpose, without overpowering your voice. Generally, there are three ways to integrate sources: summarizing, paraphrasing, and quoting. The first two take others' ideas and put them into your own words. This helps with fluidity, as a consistent voice (yours!) is maintained. However, sometimes using the author's original words is the best way to bring source information into your writing. You'll want to consider which way of integrating sources would be best for your writing.

Using Others' Words: Quoting

Directing quoting others can be very powerful, but you will want to be judicious in deciding whether or not to quote. Too many quotes can water down your writing and diminish your voice, which you don't want. Following these guidelines can help.

1. Decide whether a quote is necessary. Quotes are most useful when you are analyzing a passage, when the author has said something in such a way that you want to maintain the original language for effect, or when you want to present a source fairly and accurately and you feel that paraphrasing or summarizing won't be able to accomplish this. Sometimes as you continue drafting and revising, a quote may become less relevant than it seemed when you started writing, at which point you should consider cutting it from your work.

2. Once you have decided a quote is necessary, you need to present it in a way that makes its meaning clear to readers. Don't let a quote speak for itself by plopping it in your writing with no additional context. Writing teachers have all sorts of names for this ineffective rhetorical move; we call these "hit and run quotes" or "dropped quotes" or "dangling quotes." Instead, frame your quotation by introducing it and then explaining how it relates to what you are writing about.

Here is an example from *Comp@Central* at the end of this book:

1. "Job satisfaction is inseparably linked to how vital workers perceive their work to be, and companies can provide a boost to happiness by simply communicating a powerful central message. 'We want to do something that's bigger than ourselves and the need to earn a paycheck. Our work can give us some of that meaning when we understand the deeper why behind it,' Don Shapiro writes, underlining the massive implications of something as seemingly simple as an individual's attitude" (Peterson 73[1]).

---

[1] © Peterson

Another helpful way to think about framing your quotes is to consider them a quote sandwich.

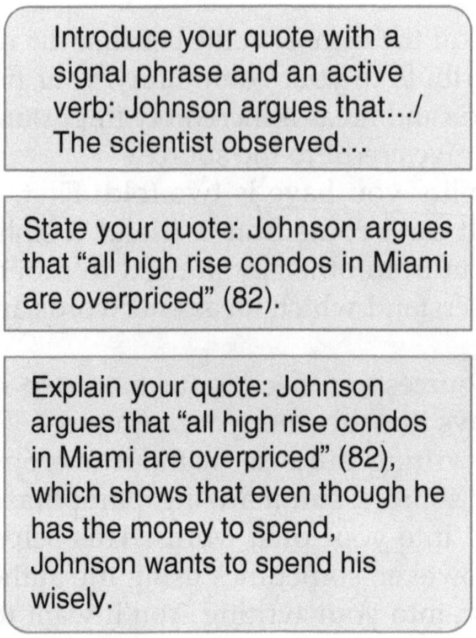

Introduce your quote with a signal phrase and an active verb: Johnson argues that…/ The scientist observed…

State your quote: Johnson argues that "all high rise condos in Miami are overpriced" (82).

Explain your quote: Johnson argues that "all high rise condos in Miami are overpriced" (82), which shows that even though he has the money to spend, Johnson wants to spend his wisely.

Figure 5.2 An idea tree
© *Kendall Hunt Publishing Company*

Integrating Quotes

Sometimes when we work with whole quotes, we include too much and run the risk of including unrelated information which can mislead or muddy our intent. One of the ways of knowing that you are fully immersed in your subject matter and speaking clearly from your point of view is when you freely move through your conversation, weaving in one or several of the sources you have come to know and support your claims with partial quote. Notice how in this example from Cedric Westcott's essay *Bojack Horseman—Most Human Character on TV* (located in *Comp@Central* in the back of this book), Wescott seamlessly weaves his source into his conversation without relying on his source to speak for him:

"In Emily Nussbaum's (2018) *New Yorker* article "The Bleakness and Joy of 'BoJack Horseman'," she references the show's 'built-in risk,' writing 'as effective as BoJack is as a character, he runs in circles. That's what addiction is, after all.' As much as BoJack wants to right the wrongs that he is responsible for, he continuously tries to escape his pain time and time again . . ." (4^2)

What Wescott is doing here is somewhat different than integrating a whole quote, rather, Wescott is utilizing partial quotations as they come to mind and relate to the syntax of his sentence. Notice how the author is still introducing his quote or set of partial quotes and afterwards explaining them, however this time the quotes explained work as a group. In fact, in many cases a partial quote or series of partial quotes is all that you will need to integrate your sources as evidence to your claims. (This topic is also covered in Getting to Writing).

Putting Others' Ideas In Your Own Words: Summarizing & Paraphrasing

Writing an effective **summary** is a balancing act. You must maintain accuracy—describing what the author has said—while also emphasizing the aspects of the text that are useful to you and your purpose. Summarizes are concise and focus on main ideas. Generally, they are all in your words rather than quoting from the author.

[2] © Cedric Westcott

Paraphrasing is similar to summary in that you are putting a source's ideas into your own words. While quoting is using the exact words and summary is an overview of the main ideas, paraphrasing utilizes a segment of the text as a means to focus on some of the details.
Steps to a good paraphrase:

1. Read your passage carefully and make sure you understand it. You won't be able to craft a solid paraphrase unless you truly understand the information you are paraphrasing.

2. Even though you have put the source's information in your own words, cite the source in your paraphrase.

3. Review your paraphrase to ensure you are not using the same words and sentence structure as the source (quote). While some overlap in vocabulary may be necessary, if you are simply replacing a few words or moving phrases around, your paraphrase is likely too similar to the original source and this is plagiarism.

Exercise

To practice your paraphrasing skills, consider the three passages below each one taken from one of three essays Comp@Central in the back of this book. You can do this exercise as a group, to compare responses to one passage, or as an individual to prepare responses to all three passages for practice. Remember that you are beginning with a passage that is a direct quote (exact words), so your job is to put the author's words into your own words without quoting and without summarizing.

1. "One of the problems in Hollywood is that many times when they're casting someone for an upcoming movie or show that has a transgender character, cisgender actors are usually the first to get considered for the role. It's not just transgender actors losing potential acting opportunities. This is happening with other sexualities and genders in the LGBTQ+ spectrum too" (Gonzales 30[3]).

2. "While the opposition claims that the information on the withdrawal plan was too public, that we needed to maintain a presence to ensure the Afghan government did not fall, and that we should not have trusted the Taliban to not allow terrorist groups to take haven in the country, these arguments are not strong enough to rationalize our physical presence in Afghanistan" (Saindon 55[4]).

3. "It is extremely difficult for someone in a state of caution to effectively evaluate benefits and drawbacks and for a valid decision. In turn, ideas can be easily misinterpreted and the wrong actions can be taken. This problem can prevent someone from growing academically as they focus too much on irrelevant details and struggle to grasp main concepts" (Klem 83[5]).

Incorporating Signal Phrases

Signal phrases serve a basic function in summaries, paraphrases, and quotes: they let readers know that information from a source is coming, usually by incorporating a verb, or a verb phrase. They can also be used to elevate the sophistication of your writing. You could introduce your source material by writing "he wrote" or "she talks about," but those verbs do not actually say anything about what the author is actually doing. Instead, if you choose signal verbs that fit the action, such as "he concedes" or "she contradicts," you will further clarify what is actually happening in the text and more accurately summarize the author's position. (This topic is also covered in Writing Processes.)

---

[3] © Nicole Gonzalez

[4] © Aaron Saindon

[5] © Erica Klem

Signal Verb Chart:

Verbs for Making an Argument
argue, assert, claim, emphasize, illustrates, implies, insist, observe, remind, report, suggest
Verbs for Agreeing
acknowledge, admit, agree, concede, corroborate, endorse, extol, praise, reaffirm, support, verify
Verbs for Disagreeing
Contend, contradict, disputes, qualify, question, refute, reject, renounce
Verbs for Recommending
advocate, demand, encourage, implore, plead, recommend, urge

Sample summary with signal verbs highlighted: In her review of *The Giving Tree* in *The New York Times Sunday Book Review,* Anna Holmes **admits** that she has never liked the book and **cites** copious online comments as evidence to demonstrate she is not alone in her disdain. She rapid-fire **previews** various readings of the text and openly **mocks** those who seek to frame the story as a bittersweet, emotional depiction of parenting or a realistic look at human nature, though she **concedes** that she could understand how readers might view the book as a cautionary tale about consumerism and consumption. Ultimately, it is clear Holmes **places** very little value in others' readings and is generally **enraged** by what she **deems** a terrible story.

Documenting Sources

How you document your sources will depend on the style your instructor has requested that you use. Some instructors will allow a variety of formats such as MLA, APA or Chicago, because writing is not just for English Studies students anymore. In other words, as different disciplines use different styles, your instructor may allow you the option of documenting your sources in a style more common within your major. Please remember that your documentation should follow the guidelines of that style only.

When you, with the guidance of your instructor, have chosen a style, then you may refer to one of the valuable, reliable and reputable websites such as Purdue Owl (https://owl.purdue.edu/) for the detailed guidelines in documenting your sources.

While it is true that you can use a tool such as EasyBib, many of these citation writers prove incomplete and/or inaccurate as they are only as good as the information you provide them. It is common at this stage of your learning for students to take the time to walk through the basics of a particular document style. With consistent use, you will begin to "think" in your chosen style and the arrangement of your information for citations will come more naturally. Then you may be able to use a citation writer as a tool as you will be prepared to check for inaccuracies before submitting your final draft.

CHAPTER 6

The 105P Workshop

by Jesskya Scoppetta

What Is 105P?

As a student in Writing 105P, you might be wondering just what this "extra" class is, and we're here to answer your questions. Writing 105P is a companion course that offers you extra practice, individualized attention, and supplemental content to help you meet the learning outcomes for your Writing 105/110 class. You might think of Writing 105P as a writing lab or workshop. Each of you was placed in 105P because your writing placement scores indicated that you are ready for WRT 110 but would benefit from some additional attention to your writing, and that is what the class offers. While the activities in 105P differ from section to section based on who your professor is, you can expect to have some combination of following:

- Time for questions left over from the 105/110 class;
- Discussion of ideas for 105/110 papers;
- Individual professor conferences for paper drafts;
- Peer-review of paper drafts;
- Individual writing time, with your instructor available for consultation and support;
- Additional content through workshops, discussion, or lecture that enhance your learning in 105/110;
- Preparation for 105/110 class, perhaps through designated reading time or exploratory writing prompts;
- Work on grammar, punctuation, and style;
- Discussion of how to succeed as a college student;
- Discussion of questions, concerns, and/or issues in 105/110 or 105P, raised by either students or the professor.

But regardless of how your 105P is set up on a day-to-day basis, your time in 105P is an opportunity to help you develop strong writing practices and habits that will help you succeed this semester and beyond. For instance, say you have been assigned an argumentative paper in 105/110 and your professor has told everyone they must draft a thesis statement. In 105P, you might be given time to workshop your thesis in class, and then have an opportunity to share it with a classmate and get feedback from that classmate before also sharing it with your professor who will provide feedback too. In this way, 105P offers an intentionally methodical and supportive environment to engage in your writing process, more than if you took 105/110 alone.

How Can I Make the Most of My 105P Class?

The following sections include a brief description of several concrete actions you can take to prepare for success in 105P. In each section, there are also "Food for Thought" activities. These are suggested reflective activities that will put into practice each of the actions. You may find your instructor will use some or all of these exercises in your 105P class. But even if your instructor does not use them, you are welcome to complete the exercises yourself as a way to help you enhance your 105P experience and help you to become the most effective writer you can be.

Ask Questions

Use 105P as an opportunity to find your voice and get answers to questions you have about your papers, assignments, readings, ideas, grammar, citation, course procedures and CCSU resources. 105P has no more than 10 students, so it offers a very small group setting. Use this structure to your advantage. It is not often that you have built-in individual time with your professor and the chance to build a small learning community with your classmates where you can have student-led conversations. To give you a few examples, questions might look like this:

- I'm confused about the assignment. Can you go over what you mean by "connect to audience and purpose?"
- Teachers have always told me to eliminate my use of the passive voice, but what does that mean? How do I fix it in my writing?
- Where is the writing center and how do I make an appointment?
- I'm having trouble finding sources for my research paper. Can you conference with me?
- I know we have to read this essay for Monday, but I can't find it on Blackboard. Will you go through where to find course materials again?
- I'm really struggling with offering an "other side" argument in my paper. Can you and I brainstorm together?
- I read the article for 105/110, but I don't understand what the author's main point is. Can we talk about it some more?
- I'm concerned about registration for next semester. Has anyone else met with their adviser?

The bottom line is: Don't be afraid to ask questions. Your professor won't know what is on your mind unless you speak up. And chances are, if you have a question, some of your classmates might have the same question and that can lead to productive discussion or additional instruction that would benefit everyone.

Food for Thought: Habits of Mind Exercise

Carefully read through a document from your 105/110 class. It could be your 105/110 syllabus, an assignment sheet, an essay, lecture slides, Blackboard postings, or your class notes. Then, write down at least one question you have and make it a goal to ask your professor your question at your next 105P meeting.

Develop Habits of Mind

Habits of mind are ways of thinking or engaging with the world around you. Identifying these practices can help you to recognize and develop characteristics that would be useful to you in your learning. In 2011, a group of writing instructors both at the college and high school levels got together and created a list of eight habits of mind that they believed would help students to succeed when writing at the college level. This framework, called the Framework for Success in Postsecondary Writing, has been endorsed by many writing teachers. These habits of mind are:

- Curiosity – the desire to know more about the world.
- Openness – the willingness to consider new ways of being and thinking in the world.
- Engagement – a sense of investment and involvement in learning.
- Creativity – the ability to use novel approaches for generating, investigating, and representing ideas.
- Persistence – the ability to sustain interest in and attention to short- and long-term projects.
- Responsibility – the ability to take ownership of one's actions and understand the consequences of those actions for oneself and others.
- Flexibility – the ability to adapt to situations, expectations, or demands.
- Metacognition – the ability to reflect on one's own thinking as well as on the individual and cultural processes used to structure knowledge

Citation: Framework for Success in Postsecondary Writing (2011) by the Council of Writing Program Administrators (CWPA), the National Council of Teachers of English (NCTE), and the National Writing Project (NWP).

Now that you have this list, you can use this information to find out more about yourself as a writer. You probably already possess some of these qualities, but may have not considered how they would be useful in a writing class or another academic setting. Or maybe you see an ability on this list that you would like to cultivate. Naming these habits and considering them allows you space to be thoughtful about how you practice them in your life. The idea here is that these characteristics or abilities are not simply something one has or does not. You have the opportunity to develop them and 105P can be the place to do it.

Food for Thought: Habits of Mind Exercise

Review the eight habits of mind and consider what these habits look like in practice in a writing class. Then, choose one habit to actively work on in your writing class. Which habit did you choose and why? How will you develop this way of approaching your learning when writing? Try to be as specific as possible. For instance, if you would like to foster persistence when you write, you will want to think about what persistence looks like in a writing class. Does it mean you dedicate more time to reading challenging texts? Or would it be seeking feedback from the writing center or your professor at multiple points during a writing assignment in order to continue to refine your writing? Or maybe you commit to completing each writing assignment, even if demands on your time make it difficult or you find the workload challenging. These are just some of the ways you might engage in your writing classes to help strengthen your ability to persist.

Engage in Reflective Practices

One way to practice the eighth habit of mind, metacognition, is to engage in reflection. Reflection asks you to learn from your experiences and become better aware of yourself as a thinker and learner. If you engage authentically in reflection, doing so can help you to better understand and retain what you are learning. It can sometimes be easy to dismiss reflective work as fluff or just journaling about your thoughts and feelings. But good reflective practices involve critically analyzing or examining an experience or process and then discussing its impact. Simply put: reflection is thinking about your *thinking* (or your actions), but for a purpose. And that purpose is to learn! Because reflection asks you to consider events or thoughts in the past, you have the time and space to think about what happened, how you felt about it, what worked or what didn't, and what you might change or improve in the future.

Often in 105P you will be asked to review and reflect upon your writing and writing process, and this reflective writing can take many forms. Your professor may incorporate reflection by asking you to do short free writes or include self-assessments when submitting drafts. Other instructors may incorporate longer, more in-depth reflective writing such as a writing portfolio cover letter or an end of semester reflective project. Engaging in the short reflection exercise below is one way you could practice reflective writing and hone your writing process to be more effective.

Food for Thought: Reflection Exercise

Free write about your writing process. Now, identify something about your writing process that you think you could change to be more effective. For example, are you a procrastinator? Do you write the paper and hit send, skipping proofreading and editing? Do you feel like your writing is all over the place and wish you took more time to organize your ideas? Make a plan and implement the change for your next 105/110 writing assignment. After the paper has been turned in, consider your experience and write it up. What did you change? Why did you change it? What are your thoughts on the outcome of the change? Is this a permanent change you will make? Or did your efforts not make much of a difference?

Build Your Critical Reading Toolkit

Reading and writing go hand in hand. If you want to become a better writer, one of the most effective steps you can take is to up your reading game. Simply spending more time reading texts of all kinds can be useful: the more you read, the better your vocabulary becomes. Additionally, frequent reading means increased exposure to different genres and writers and more models of how other writers tackle their subjects. But there are also critical reading practices that help you maximize your engagement with texts so you better understand them and can therefore write more confidently about them. Below are just a few common critical reading practices. Some of these may be useful to you, while others might not. The point is to find strategies that work for you and add them to your toolkit.

Annotation

Annotation is a fancy word for saying taking notes. Annotations are any markings you make as you are reading a text, including full sentence comments and questions; shorthand notes like !!! or ??? or ☺; circled words; and underlined or highlighted terms, just to name a few examples. Taking notes, in whatever form, is useful for a variety of reasons. First, taking the time to mark up a text with your comments, questions, reactions, and notes helps you to better understand a piece of writing as it forces you to slow down and engage with the ideas presented in the text. Additionally, it gives you something to say. Readers who annotate well have ready-made questions and/or points for class discussion. Finally, these interactions with the text can be prep for writing on a paper, as this is your initial interaction with the author and their ideas. Often these notes can serve as the basis for a more comprehensive response once it is time to get writing.

Here is an example of an annotated page of Maslin Laberge's "Rhetorical Analysis of Kenneth Goldsmith"[1]:

---

[1] © Maslin Laberge

Rhetorical Analysis of Kenneth Goldsmith

Maslin Laberge, Writing 110

It's likely that when *Homo habilis* sharpened the first stick into a spear, one of his fellow cavemen complained about the good old days when clubs were all they needed. In the countless millennia since, human technology progressed considerably, always with similar debates about its use. In his article, "Go Ahead: Waste Time on the Internet", Kenneth Goldsmith advocates for the titular message. He argues that 'The Internet' is not a singular beast, but countless different things for different people (and even for the same person). Considering that this entity can serve almost any purpose, it cannot be generalized that being on the internet is wasting time. He brings up numerous oft-spoken criticisms towards being online and points out how they don't stand up to scrutiny and how the nay-sayers don't acknowledge the usefulness. Goldsmith's use of tone and logos provide a compelling argument that time on the internet is not wasted but this could have been strengthened with a stronger use of ethos.

ha, ha ☺ funny opening line

summary of goldsmith's ideas or the "they say"

writer's thesis

appeals to logic or authors arguments

— appeals to author's credibility

Goldsmith's article was first published in mid 2016 for the *Los Angeles Times*. As implied above, he seeks to alter opinions by providing reasons why the internet is not a waste of time. The general attitude towards the internet in 2016 is fundamentally the same as today. In the developed world, everyone except Luddites and the Amish make use of it and it's effects reach them regardless. More specifically, Goldsmith is referring to

→ Is it, though? Or has the pandemic shifted it?

Luddites - people opposed to new technology

Goldsmith's article was first published in mid-2016 for the *Los Angeles Times*. As implied above, he seeks to alter opinions by providing reasons why the internet is not a waste of time. The general attitude toward the internet in 2016 is fundamentally the same as today. In the developed world, everyone except Luddites and the Amish make use of it and it's effects reach them regardless. More specifically, Goldsmith is referring to casual usage: portable devices, social media, and web browsing, which is the typical consumer's engagement. These are all things any reader would be familiar with, particularly the adults who would be reading the *L.A. Times* who consider their children/friend/colleague to be always online and wasting their time. Due to the assumed familiarity of anyone reading, Goldsmith is able to take a more casual tone throughout the essay, providing relatively simple arguments that the readers will be able to understand and hopefully relate to.

Believing/Doubting Game

Writing scholar Peter Elbow is credited with this idea called the Believing and Doubting game. The concept is simple: in order to better understand a piece of writing, you want to look at it through two opposing viewpoints. First, consider yourself someone who believes the text and think about all the reasons to support this point of view. List any evidence that bolsters this position. Welcome and trust the author and the argument. Then, review the text again, but as someone who doubts, or critically interrogates it. Be a skeptical reader and look for issues with the evidence presented, the author's logic, and contradictions in the essay. Ask yourself, what issues or problems do I see with this point of view? This critical reading strategy can be especially helpful if you are trying to choose or assess a position. It can help you hone not only what others believe, but what you believe as well. The idea for the game is simple, but the act of switching viewpoints can be more difficult than you might expect!

Reading Rhetorically

If you're not sure yet what rhetoric or reading rhetorically means, that's okay. The Introduction to this textbook has more to say about rhetoric, but we'll offer a brief explanation here: rhetoric is the art of effective writing or speaking. So, reading rhetorically means looking at the choices a writer makes and analyzing the effectiveness of these choices. When reading rhetorically, you will want to consider questions about who the target audience is, what the author's purpose is, and who the author is. What is the author's goal? What are they responding to? What is motivating them? Who is the writer's intended audience? What choices is the writer making to reach their audience? Thinking about these questions when you sit down to read (and taking notes on your observations), are easy ways to incorporate reading rhetorically into your reading practices. Doing this will help you to understand not only what a text says (the summary of ideas presented), but *how* those ideas function within the text to create an effective argument.

Food for Thought: Critical Reading Exercise

Next time you have to read a text for your 105/110 class, try one of the critical reading strategies listed above. After, reflect on the experience. How did it go giving this strategy a try? What was useful about this strategy? What wasn't useful? Would you add this strategy to your toolkit? Why or why not?

Exit Interview: Now That You Have Completed First-Year Writing, What Comes Next?

by James P. Austin

As we have stated throughout this book, the purpose of first-year writing is to help prepare you for the demands and expectations of college-level writing. As you complete your first-year writing course and begin to look ahead, there is a new question: What will college writing look like in your future courses?

The answer, in part, is that *it depends*. What does it depend upon? Mainly, it concerns the academic discipline or professional field you will select as your major. *Writing in the disciplines or professions* is more diverse and complex than first-year writing, because the writing you will be asked to do will be specific to the discipline or major that will become your primary focus. In this chapter, we will refer to all such work *writing in the major*.

To successfully apply what you have learned in first-year writing onto writing in the major, you will need to first generalize concepts of rhetoric and genre you have learned throughout first- year writing. This means that you first should consider these concepts applicable to any writing situation and major, and not just for the writing you have done in first-year writing.

As far as rhetorical concepts go, it will be important to gain a strong understanding of your *audience for writing in your major*. Audiences in writing in the major are very specific: they are members of an academic community, or seasoned professionals. They are knowledgeable and credible (that's right—ethos again). They are well-read and often boast significant experience. They often care deeply about their chosen focus area, and they will expect you to write at a level which shows deeper engagement with concepts and practices of a chosen field. This will help you establish *ethos*. You need to address them with respect but also in a manner that shows knowledge of rhetorical and genre concepts as applied to the major.

Because of this challenge, it is critical to refine *the purpose(s) for your writing*. If, for example, your purpose is to persuade your audience through reasoned argument, you need to understand what it will take to persuade a more specialized audience. What kind of evidence will be compelling to them? Do they value more recent evidence, or more established sources? What kinds of journals and other publications are appropriate for your purpose?

A Quick Aside

You may have noticed that many of the concepts you have learned about in this book, such as those pertaining to rhetoric and genre, are being used more interchangeably throughout the book. This is because concepts in rhetorical and genre theory speak to one another and, thus, are interdependent. As you become more capable with identifying and using these concepts, you may also make connections between them that you were not able to do at first. For example, when I discussed *audience* above, I also addressed *ethos*. This is because one must take audience into account when establishing ethos. Why? Because the authority and trustworthiness of the communicator is partially dependent upon the needs of the rhetorical situation, such as the audience you are addressing. Because of this, it is more challenging—and potentially rewarding—to address a specialized academic audience in your major, rather than the more general academic audience you may have imagined in first-year writing.

Back to Regular Programming

Likewise, the *exigence* and *constraints* of your rhetorical situation have also changed. In the minds of some student writers, the exigence is often provided by the instructor: we assign the work, and you are motivated to complete writing assignments for a grade and/or to learn course content. While this may remain true in some regards as you move forward, you will likely discover that the "external" exigence—that is, motives provide by someone else—is replaced by "intrinsic" exigence—that is, your own desire to communicate and learn in more advanced ways to specialized audiences, which will pertain much more directly to a career path. As you take on the specialized work in your major, you may begin to consider applying for internships; you may visualize potential career paths; you may want to pursue increasingly specialized education in graduate school. This means that you are beginning to see your education, and your writing development, in a new light. As such, your motivation will mature. Likewise, the situational constraints will become clearer as you become more familiar with the writing expectations in your major and beyond. There are simply aspects of writing situations that you cannot change, that you must work with or work around.

Upshot: Practical Implications

What this means is that you will continue to write (and more broadly, to communicate) well into your future in education and beyond. What do you need to consider when you encounter future writing situations? We have already started down that path, in a way: you will need to account for more specialized contexts and expectations as you proceed through college. In this section, I would like to expand on this and offer some practice "rules of the road" you will encounter in the future.

Rhetorically Speaking...

You will need to be aware of the *purpose* for more specialized writing assignments, especially as they pertain to *systems of activity* in a specialized major or profession. One writing assignment may become part of a chain of writing assignments that have a logical relationship to one another and contributes to the completion of a complex task, such as preparing for a presentation or capstone project; in this way, purpose is defined, in part, through the way any one writing task satisfies both its own purpose and contributes within a complex chain of activity carried out through several means, including writing, toward the sat. That is, one writing task may be only a piece of a larger project; knowing where one writing task "fits", and what purpose it is meant to achieve within the activity system, will help satisfy the purpose for larger and more complex projects through the writing that you do.

Likewise, you will need to consider *audiences* in different ways. In college writing, your instructor is always one of your audiences. However, as you write in more specialized ways, your instructor's role as audience is likely to change. Remember, your instructors are highly educated, highly specialized experts who are active and likely are published in their academic disciplines. Your instructors are likely to read as members of their academic discipline or professional community as you enter the upper division courses designed to develop abilities (including writing abilities). As such, you are being inculcated into an academic discipline or professional community because you will be instructed in specialized forms of communication and expected to learn how to write *as* members of that discipline or community *to other members of that discipline or community.*

To communicate effectively to members of a discipline or community you are seeking to join, your own credibility and authority—your *ethos*—is critical. As yourself: how does one comport themselves as credible in specialized contexts? What does it mean to be knowledgeable in such contexts? Is it appropriate, for example, to begin a writing task with a *pathos*-infused narrative approach? Or would such a choice be inappropriate?

Call and Response: The Relationship of Rhetoric to Genre

Amy Braziller and Elizabeth Kleinfeld, the authors of *The Bedford Book of Genres* (2021) note that "genres respond to rhetorical situations" (p. 29). Effective communication occurs when the type of writing (genre) we employ is an appropriate match for the expectations of the rhetorical situation, which focuses especially on purpose, audience, constraints, and Kairos. (Some of what I express below is influenced by their text.)

As such, to fully understand and apply the new rhetorical challenges awaiting in your major, we also must account for important considerations in the related area of *genre*: the typical and accepted responses to writing situations. As you move beyond first-year writing and begin to encounter writing tasks in your major, the genres you will compose also will change—in some respects, drastically.

One major aspect of any genre is its *common elements*—what is it about an essay for a social sciences course that distinguishes it from a lab report for a biology course (and vice versa)? What differentiates writing for an engineering course from that of a business course, or nursing from social work? It is often useful to examine several versions of specialized genres as you gain an understanding of the common elements of any specialized genre. However, simply examining genres and attempting to imitate them will get you only so far unless you know what you should look for.

An important consideration is the *writing style* of a genre. While you may have developed a sense of writing in an academic style in your first-year writing courses, you must continually assess what kinds of writing styles are appropriate for the genres you will compose for more specialized audiences. For example, should the writing style be straightforward and concise? Is passive voice appropriate? How long and complex are the sentences? Should the style include the presence of the author—that is, should we be aware of the specific individual, or should the writing appear objective as without any subjective presence?

Additionally, consider the *design* and other formal aspects of the genre. Does a genre include headings and sub-headings, figures, and tables? What about footnotes or endnotes? What citation format is followed? Understanding the design aspects is also an important aspect of writing successfully in your major.

Finally, what counts as effective *sources* in your major and/or professional setting? You have been given a foundational background in academic sources; however, your major may have specific expectations for the kinds of academic sources you should use. Is there a particular type of research database you should be using which is most relevant to your major area? What counts as credible—qualitative research which presents findings from interviews, focus groups, or surveys? Or quantitative research which processes large amounts of data to express large trends over time? Is archival research important, or does your major value recent data or original research? Understanding what counts as most credible in your chosen major will guide you toward the databases and other research and data platforms appropriate for your major.

One More Thing...

Throughout this textbook, you have not only learned important concepts and practices important to your development into a college-level writer, but you have actually used writing many times as a method of learning. The noted writing scholar Peter Elbow (1997) gave a term to this approach: low stakes writing. This writing is "often ungraded and may receive little or no feedback from instructors" (Palmquist 2020, p. 11). Why then, one might ask would a student write anything if it isn't going to be graded by an instructor? If you have that question, it is a very good one. Low-stakes writing is a "tool for learning rather than a test of learning for writers explain concepts or ideas to themselves, to ask questions, to make connections" (McLeod & Maimon 2000, p. 579). Such writing can include:

- brainstorming
- summarizing and responding to readings
- reflecting on class sessions
- defining concepts and describing processes
- listing important ideas and questions about a subject
- mapping and clustering
- developing outlines

There is some debate about whether these approaches to low-stakes writing can be useful for students who are learning to write in their major. Our position in this area says *yes*, this work is an important part of writing in the major. You will need to brainstorm ideas to see how well you understand them. Eventually, you will apply what you learn on more advanced concepts and forms of analysis. You will need to summarize and respond to specialized readings and prepare yourself for class, just as you will need to define specialized concepts, processes, and practices; you may need to visualize connections through mapping, clustering, and outlining. This "low stakes" approach can not only help you explain to yourself what you are learning, but to *identify the limits of what you know, understand, and can do without assistance* so that you can better know where and when you need the assistance of a more capable peer, an instructor, or the Writing Center. In this respect, "low stakes writing" is not just "for you"—it helps you to figure out what actions you need to take, what resources you should access, to better understand and apply expectations within your academic discipline, including writing in the major.

It's Not Goodbye: It's See You Soon

As you close out your first-year writing experience, remember that you will continue to grow and develop as a writer and, more broadly, as a communicator throughout your academic and professional careers. That means that you are not done writing—far from it. Learning how to communicate effectively in many situations and to many audiences will serve you extremely well into the future. What you have learned in first-year writing has provided you with a foundation which you can carry with you into your writing in the major. The work you do in those courses will set you up for further and more complex and demanding academic and professional communication. We wish you all success in your next steps, and congratulations for completing first-year writing at CCSU.

References

Braziller, Amy, and Elizabeth Kleinfeld. *The Bedford Book of Genres: A Guide and Reader*. Bedford/St. Martin's, 2021.

Elbow, Peter. "High Stakes and Low Stakes in Responding to Student Writing." *New Directions for Teaching and Learning*, Vol. 69, 1997, pp. 5–13.

McLeod, Susan H., and Elaine Maimon. "Clearing the Air: WAC Myths and Realities." *College English*, Vol. 62, no. 5, 2000, pp. 573–583. https://www.jstor.com/stable/378962.

Palmquist, Mike. "A Middle Way for WAC: Writing to Engage." *The WAC Journal,* Vol. 31, 2020, https://doi.org/10.37514/WAC-J.2020.31.1.01.

Student Essays

Bojack Horseman—Most Human Character on TV

Scrolling through Netflix late at night, it would at first glance be difficult to distinguish animated adult comedy *Bojack Horseman* from the seemingly endless supply of formulaic, bland, and often tone-deaf animated comedies that plague the streaming service. *Bojack Horseman* is undeniably a comedy, and its jokes and humor alone are strong enough to catapult the show into elite comedy status—but as funny as the show is, it prioritizes detailed characters and storytelling above all else, all while still finding more than enough opportunities to make the audience laugh. Rather than showing us a constant string of barely related episodes that exist almost independently of one another (i.e. *The Simpsons*), the show's episodes are all installments in a continuous and multifaceted storyline. The show's main lead and title character (voiced by Will Arnett) is a middle-aged, half-man half-horse who formerly starred as the father in the lighthearted and beloved fictional 90's sitcom *Horsin' Around*.

The Bojack that we are introduced to from the show's very first episode is a stark contrast from the lovable character he portrayed on *Horsin' Around*. Bojack suffers from depression and is overall an extremely insecure and self-destructive character who regularly abuses drugs and alcohol. Throughout the story, we are exposed time and time again to many of Bojack's worst decisions; these are rarely just referenced briefly in the show's dialogue, but shown on screen to us, the audience. In Emily Nussbaum's (2018) *New Yorker* article "The Bleakness and Joy of "BoJack Horseman"", she references the show's "built-in risk," writing "as effective as BoJack is as a character, he runs in circles. That's what addiction is, after all." As much as Bojack wants to right the wrongs that he is responsible for, he continuously tries to escape his pain time and time again by going on alcohol or drug-fueled binges that inevitably result in even more damage to himself and others.

The COVID-19 virus has been a terrifying example of a worldwide health crisis that we can easily see the tangible symptoms of; but lurking under the surface of COVID lies a dangerous predator that is not so easily seen. In "Stupid Piece of Sh*t"—a *Bojack Horseman* episode from Season 4—we see this aspect of invisibility in mental illness portrayed with a very unique and effective approach. The episode focuses on Bojack's internal monologue (still voiced by Arnett), beginning with him lying in bed while calling himself a "Stupid piece of shit" along with other insults. Much of the episode continues in this same fashion, with Bojack mentally berating himself repeatedly and imagining unrealistically dark and negative ways that others view him. The belief and thoughts that others hate him or that they think he is a bad person only furthers his internal monologue's abuse of himself, and he tries to get away by going to bars as well as sitting in his car doing nothing for hours on end. He interacts with other characters via normal dialogue throughout the episode, but these scenes are interspersed with his own thoughts, showing the viewer how hard it can be to tell what is going on in someone's head.

While we can tell from someone's external symptoms such as coughing or high temperature that they may be physically ill, it is much harder to know when someone may be suffering internally. Mental health is an increasingly severe issue in our country, with Mental Health America (2021) citing an increase of 1.5 million adults who experienced a mental illness between 2017 and 2018. These are numbers from well before the pandemic, which has itself contributed to an even further increase in rates of depression, anxiety, and suicidal ideation according to a 2020 report by the CDC. Stigma and negative assumptions surrounding mental illness are certainly not things of the past, but there are major strides being made to help reduce them. A survey conducted by HealthPartners (2020) in Minnesota and Wisconsin in 2017 and 2019 shows that the Make It OK campaign—which seeks to educate people about mental illness and reduce the stigma surrounding it—has drastically increased the percentage of people in the observed regions that would be willing to talk about their mental illness, tell a friend if they had a mental illness, or seek help for their mental illness.

The term "mental illness" has been used numerous times throughout this essay already, but I would like to briefly clarify what it can mean. Much like the wide variation in physical illnesses, people battling mental illness are not dealing with one condition; they can be experiencing symptoms from one or more of a long list of different disorders. *Bojack Horseman*'s representation of characters with mental illness does not stop at just Bojack with his alcoholism, frequent addictions, and depression; fellow lead character Diane Nguyen, (voiced by Alison Brie) is a writer who suffers from anxiety and depression throughout the show, and Bojack's mother Beatrice (Wendie Malick) has a particularly hard to watch struggle with dementia. There is a vast range of severity and variation in disorders under the blanket term "mental illness," and these specific conditions are not mutually exclusive. Recent years have seen numerous celebrities including Demi Lovato, Dwayne "The Rock" Johnson, Billie Eilish and many more come forward with stories of their own experiences battling mental illness. Seeing and hearing celebrities that we idolize talk about their personal struggles with mental health can be an extremely powerful tool to both help those suffering to realize that they are not alone, and to show that mental illness is not about strength and can happen to anyone.

A large part of what makes *Bojack Horseman* so different from other shows or even comedies about substance abuse and mental illness can be seen immediately, from Bojack's very own appearance. Issues such as depression, anxiety, addiction, and other forms of mental illness are problems that are uniquely human. Bojack himself however—along with many other characters in the show—is very clearly not a human at all. Rather than creating a show about a middle-aged man struggling with human problems such as mental illness and addiction, this world shows us a horse with those same human problems; and the absurdity and uniqueness of this replacement of man with horseman makes the same story far more interesting. As entertaining as it may be to watch an irreverent sitcom or an emotionally moving drama, *Bojack Horseman* introduces a new layer entirely by somehow managing to be both at the same time. It is this careful tightrope walk between being a realistic, important drama about mental illness and addiction and being an absurd comedy that makes the show so different from anything else quite like it.

Characters in *Bojack Horseman* are not always what they appear, and *Time's Arrow*, one of the show's most heart-wrenching episodes late in Season 4 is a perfect example of this. The episode, being almost entirely from the perspective of Bojack's dementia-ridden mother Beatrice Horseman, is in a very different format from the majority of the show's episodes. Taking place late in season 4, Bojack's mother has until this point been portrayed as a cold, uncaring mother who played a huge part in shaping Bojack to be the damaged and emotionally scarred (horse)person that he is today. This episode displays that coldness in the older version of Beatrice, but also shows us another version of Beatrice; it shows us a younger character who once had aspirations and dreams of her own, a character whose good intentions and hope (like Bojack) eventually crumbled away after years spent in the presence of either a cruel, uncaring father or an emotionally distant husband. And the present-day version of Beatrice shows a broken character so ravaged with dementia that she can no longer even distinguish past or present. Bojack Horseman is not a show where you can easily place blanket labels such as "good" or "bad" on its characters, and this episode is one of the absolute best in the series at displaying that.

With depression, mental illness, and society's overall awareness around them having risen in recent years, it makes perfect sense that a show like *Bojack Horseman* became as popular as it is. Whether the show draws you in with its humor or its realistic and unrefined depiction of grief and depression, one cannot help but leave each episode wanting to know what will happen next. From his opioid-fueled choking of fellow costar Gina Cazador (Stephanie Beatriz) on set of a show to convincing former *Horsin' Around* costar Sarah Lynn to break her sobriety to go on a bender that ultimately leads to her death, it is no longer easy to see Bojack as the protagonist that we have come to expect most main characters on TV to be. However the audience ultimately views Bojack and the other characters by the show's end, it is rare to see a show—lest of all a comedy—provide this level of complexity to a character guilty of such horrendous actions. While Bojack is of course a fictional character, it is not hard to come up with very real examples of people who bear many similarities to the mentally ill substance abusing horseman himself.

Following the divorce of Johnny Depp and Amber Heard in 2016, an increasingly ugly and drawn-out series of court battles has gone on between the two actors stemming from Heard's allegations of abuse against Depp and the resulting article from British newspaper *The Sun,* which referred to Depp as a "wife-beater" (Marshall, 2020b). As a longtime fan of Depp's acting, a part of me would like to believe that these allegations are false and that the person whose work I have so long admired has never been violent toward Heard or other women. However, between Heard's allegations as well as the court ruling in 2020 which backed up these said allegations with "overwhelming evidence" of Depp physically assaulting Heard on twelve occasions, I find it harmful and delusional to try to claim that Depp is somehow an innocent victim defending himself as so many of his supporters continue to do. This battle between the two stars is and has been an extremely public affair, and many fans of both actors are quick to fervently defend their favorite of the two celebrities while often completely vilifying the other.

The many Johnny Depp fans who continue to blindly idolize him despite evidence of his past violence towards Heard astounds me, but this examination of the two celebrities' tumultuous and drug-addled relationship is not intended to condemn or support one or the other. Depp has claimed that often the physical altercations between himself and Heard were instigated by her rather than the other way around, with him sometimes leaving the room and trying to distance himself from Heard during arguments in an attempt to prevent the situation from escalating (Marshall, 2020a). Several of Depp's claims have themselves been supported by witness testimony, further muddying the waters on just how accountable each of the actors is for the violent incidents in their relationship.

Ultimately, it is pretty much meaningless to ask the question of whether Johnny Depp—or Bojack Horseman—is a good or bad person. Like Depp, Bojack is a famous actor who abuses alcohol, drugs, and sometimes women. Unlike in Depp's real-life situation however, in *Bojack Horseman* we as the audience see the inside information that leads to these self-destructive or otherwise harmful actions; we even see that Bojack does truly appear to be remorseful for causing Sarah Lynn's death, choking Gina, and attempting to have sex with Penny (the 17-year-old daughter of his former love interest Charlotte). His self-loathing and regret involving these actions does not excuse them or make him a more sympathetic character, but offers a rare look into the mind of an abuser that we do not get to see in real life.

Works Cited

Butler, Bethonie *"Celebrities are talking more about their own mental health. It's helping — even if it's complicated."* Washington Post, 2020

Czeisler et. al *"Mental Health, Substance Use, and Suicidal Ideation During the COVID-19 Pandemic"* 2020

HealthPartners (2020)*"Stigma of mental illnesses decreasing, survey shows"*

Hess, A. (2018). BoJack Was Made For This Moment. The New York Times., 168(58108), 1–2.

Marshall, A. (2020, July 25). A Court Battle They Could Both Lose. *New York Times*, 169(58765), C3.

Marshall, A. (2020, November 3). Johnny Depp, Called a "Wife Beater," Loses Libel Suit. *New York Times*, 170(58866), C3.

Mental Health America (2021)*"The State Of Mental Health In America"*

Nussbaum, Emily *"The Bleakness and Joy of "BoJack Horseman""* The New Yorker, August 8 & 15, issue 2016

Rhetorical Analysis of Kenneth Goldsmith

It's likely that when *Homo habilis* sharpened the first stick into a spear, one of his fellow cavemen complained about the good old days when clubs were all they needed. In the countless millennia since, human technology progressed considerably, always with similar debates about its use. In his article, "Go Ahead: Waste Time on the Internet", Kenneth Goldsmith advocates for the titular message. He argues that 'The Internet' is not a singular beast, but countless different things for different people (and even for the same person). Considering that this entity can serve almost any purpose, it cannot be generalized that being on the internet is wasting time. He brings up numerous oft-spoken criticisms towards being online and points out how they don't stand up to scrutiny and how the nay-sayers don't acknowledge the usefulness. Goldsmith's use of tone and logos provide a compelling argument that time on the internet is not wasted but this could have been strengthened with a stronger use of ethos.

Goldsmith's article was first published in mid 2016 for the *Los Angeles Times*. As implied above, he seeks to alter opinions by providing reasons why the internet is not a waste of time. The general attitude towards the internet in 2016 is fundamentally the same as today. In the developed world, everyone except Luddites and the Amish make use of it and it's effects reach them regardless. More specifically, Goldsmith is referring to casual usage: portable devices, social media, and web browsing, which is the typical consumer's engagement. These are all things any reader would be familiar with, particularly the adults who would be reading the *L.A. Times* who consider their children/friend/colleague to be always online and wasting their time. Due to the assumed familiarity of anyone reading, Goldsmith is able to take a more casual tone throughout the essay, providing relatively simple arguments that the readers will be able to understand and hopefully relate to.

Because anyone who frequently uses the web has heard the same criticisms repeated time after time, Goldsmith is able to mimic this by using a somewhat frustrated and skeptical tone. The opening in particular emphasizes this, "When I click around news sites, am I wasting time because I should be working instead? What if I've spent hours working, and I need a break? Am I wasting time if I watch cat videos, but not if I read a magazine story about the Iran nuclear deal?" (Goldsmith 500). His barrage of responses to the question of the internet being a waste of time provides immediate skepticism towards the "common knowledge" and provides examples of his point that the internet is multifaceted. Additionally, it makes him appear on the defensive, despite having arguments for his point, which feeds into the feeling of frustration. Further along, he brings up another point, "I keep reading—on screens—that in the age of screens we've lost our ability to concentrate, that we've become distracted. But when I look around me and see people riveted to their devices, I notice a great wealth of concentration, focus, and engagement." (Goldsmith 501). By emphasizing "on screens," (Goldsmith 501) he shows that even those who claim this modern technology is bad are using it to spread their arguments. This apparent contradiction helps the reader to also feel skeptical of such claims, as does Goldsmith's immediate followup, calling the point into question. This pattern of giving a common complaint and then Goldsmith arguing against it is used throughout the essay, which in addition to providing reasons for his point, gives a feeling of frustration.

Besides conveying tone, this providing of reason invokes logos, which is critical for anything but the most immaterial arguments. Naturally Goldsmith does make use of it, providing reasons why a given criticism falls short. "And I keep reading—on the Internet—that the Internet has made us antisocial, that we've lost the ability to have a conversation. But when I see people with their devices, what I see is people communicating with one another: texting, chatting, IM'ing" (Goldsmith 501). He provides a common objection to being online and gives rationale as to why the reader should doubt it. However, his use of logos couldn't be considered flawless. As shown by the previous quote, Goldsmith uses anecdotal evidence for his arguments, rather than rigorous logic and scientific studies. This does serve to make the article more approachable for the general public which it was written for. Furthermore, while anecdotes may be outside the realm of pure logic, they're still evidence. Because internet usage is omnipresent for any reader, they could also look at people in public or ask their friends and potentially have Goldsmith's beliefs about it's flexibility affirmed.

Related to the topic of anecdotes vs formal studies is ethos and Goldsmith's use of it. As previously stated, ethos is used fairly weakly. Goldsmith's casual tone and personal anecdotes invokes the feeling of an acquaintance giving their opinion. While this makes his essay readable for anyone with a copy of the *L.A. Times* or his book, it doesn't provide a reason why he would necessarily be correct. His credentials are only mentioned in the author blurb rather than the work itself, which may not have been present in the original publication. Goldsmith does provide a quote from Marshall McLuhan which helps his point, but fails to mention McLuhan's credentials as a modern philosopher. If he had added a reference to a formal study that casual usage of the internet can help with reading or communication skills (just as an example), then readers would have more reason to trust his overall statement that the internet isn't a waste of time.

Goldsmith additionally makes use of pathos, although perhaps not as frequently. If the reader has a preexisting attachment to using the internet, then any argument in it's favor would feed off of that and strengthen Goldsmith's argument. However, such readers wouldn't be the ones who need convincing. Goldsmith dismisses the emotional appeal that internet critics uses, but uses it himself several paragraphs later "After reading one of those hysterical "devices are ruining your child" articles... The daughter responded indignantly that she wasn't just 'clicking around.' She was connecting with a community of girls her own age who shared similar interests," (Goldsmith 503). His use of the word hysterical shows that the opposing article should be ignored, while his reasoning gives his argument value. Goldsmith's use of logic makes his use of "think of the children" stronger than the one he's criticizing, allowing use to turn this cliche emotional appeal for himself.

Overall, Goldsmith's skeptical tone makes his writing more casual, which fits the general audience it was presented to. This also means his arguments aren't as hurt by the lack of hard evidence. Goldsmith's use of tone and logos provide a solid argument that the internet shouldn't be considered a waste of time, but a greater use of ethos would provide more reason to trust him. All of these parts allow him to persuasively present his argument in a way that's entertaining to read.

Works Cited

Goldsmith, Kenneth."Go Ahead: Waste time on the Internet". *"They Say/I Say" The Moves That Matter in Academic Writing With Readings*, Edited by Marilyn Moller, W.W. Norton & Company, Inc, 2021, pp. 582–586.

What It Means to Represent Transgender Identities on Television

For the past decade, members of the LGBTQ are being represented more than ever in mainstream media like television. There has been a significant correlation in the increase of LGBTQ representation and LGBTQ acceptance in our society. More people, whether they identify as part of this community or not, have been more open-minded and accept people with different sexualities and genders. As our society becomes more tolerant, it provides a space for people to express their sexual and gender identities more freely. In a recent study by Gallup (a company that develops public opinion polls), it showed that as of 2021, 5.6% of Americans identify as LGBTQ compared to the 3.5% in 2012.

Every year, we see more and more representation from this community as they are finally being given a spotlight in popular media like shows, movies, and music. Before, queer topics couldn't be brought up as openly as they are now because they were seen as taboo. Now, queer topics can be talked about like it's the norm, which is how it should be. According to GLAAD's (Gay & Lesbian Allegiance Against Defamation) "Where We Are on TV" report (2020), 10.2% of regular characters on television identify as LGBTQ in 2019-2020. It was recorded as the highest percentage of representation for the LGBTQ+ community as of today. This is a massive jump from where it used to be. In 2005-2006, there was less than 2% of LGBTQ+ representation on TV. We also have more queer musical artists in the top music charts like Lil Nas X, an openly gay multiplatinum singer and rapper, who has recently released an album about his life and what it's like to be queer in the music industry. His most recent trending music video depicted him having romantic and sexual relations with a male football player for his song "That's What I Want," with over 55 million views on YouTube. The ability to release a music video like that without backlash from the majority of the media is significantly different to how it was in the 80's. When Queen, the rock band, released their music video for "I Want To Break Free," their music video was banned in North America by MTV because they were dressed in drag. Queer content is widely more accepted in today's society than it has been in the past couple of decades.

Presenting LGBTQ+ content in popular media is important for our culture because it gives a voice to the people who have been prejudiced and discriminated against for centuries. A recent study by Fandom.com (2020) found that audiences are using entertainment as a way to connect with other people. Representing the LGBTQ+ community in popular media allows people to understand themselves and others, which creates a positive impact in how people interact in our society. According to UCLA's Williams Institute (Flores, 2021), 131 out of the 174 countries they have studied have experienced increased acceptance of LGBTQ+ people since 1981. The remaining countries either faced a decline or remained the same. The year 1981 is significant because that was the year when the first cases of AIDS began to appear in the U.S. When people discovered that the majority of AIDS cases were gay or bisexual men, there was strong sense of homophobia in the country. President Ronald Reagan's administration remained quiet and provided little to no funding towards AIDS relief, costing the lives of thousands of Americans. Reagan's advisor at the time even called the epidemic as "nature's revenge on gay men" (White, 2004). Most of the homophobia towards victims and members of the LGBTQ+ community at the time stemmed from the fact that there wasn't enough information that would help people understand what it was. This fear caused people to look at AIDS as a "gay disease" and alienated queer people. Fortunately, we now have more research studies and medications that help those who are affected.

It's exciting that the LGBTQ+ community has been steadily getting more representation on TV over the years. Gay and lesbian characters are now regularly appearing on shows and movies. Transgender identities are regularly being shown on television as well, however, it is not as frequent as gays and lesbians. Even though they've been around for centuries, there still seems to be issues with getting realistic depictions of these gender identities that don't involve harmful stereotypes. Another problem is that when there are shows or movies that involve a transgender character, the role is usually given to cisgender actor. Even if the actor has good intentions, this still causes a problem with misrepresentation for the community.

While there has been a rise in transgender representation in popular media, transgender identities are still being underrepresented compared to gays and lesbians on television. The other problem is that they're also being misrepresented when transgender characters are written based on stigmatizing stereotypes. If you're looking for good transgender content in shows or movies from the past two decades, there isn't a very long list. Positive representations for this community have come a long way, but there's still a history of the negative representations that they've had to endure that are still out there today. Content from the early 2000's were either documentaries about the transgender community or media that contained offensive content against trans people. In GLAAD's 2002 television report, 54% of the 102 episodes that included transgender characters on TV were categorized as containing negative depictions.

These depictions often ranged from having the transgender character be cast as victims, sex workers, murderers, or villains. In the same research study, they also found that "anti-transgender slurs, language and dialogue was present in at least 61% of the catalogued episodes and storylines." An example of this would be in an episode by the popular animated show, *The Cleveland Show*, where one of the characters projectile vomits for a long period of time after discovering that he had slept with a transgender woman. The episode also had defamatory characterizations and anti trans language. Another show is *CSI*. One of their first reoccurring villains was a transgender serial killer who steals his dead father's identity, murders his own mother, and who later commits suicide. There's also instances where the main characters of the show would openly mock the bodies of transgender murder victims. Then there's the series, *Nip/Tuck*, where they feature a character who regrets her transition, a transgender sex worker who gets beaten, and an entire season arc dedicated to a psychotic transgender pedophile that sleeps with her own son. Depictions like these can instill harmful ideas that transgender people should be feared or that they are mentally ill.

Fortunately, we have become more progressive as a society and have reduced the amount of negative content we see now. While the steady increase and frequency in "positive" or non offensive content of transgender on television is good, what's more important is the progress we've made in depicting them as real people. When I say real, I mean trans characters that are complex and that have depth. Characters that aren't just there for shock purposes but that provide something to the show or movie's storyline. Characters whose narratives aren't just built around discovering their identity, but about other things in the story. In FX's show, *Pose*, this was shown in all their characters.

Pose is an exemplar show that has rightfully earned the respect and adoration of the LGBTQ+ community not only for its incredible storyline and actors, but for the way they positively represented the transgender community. It is a drama series set in the 1980's that explores what life and society was like in New York when you're queer. One of the main story arcs in the show was the fight against HIV/AIDS. It provides an emotional insight into the community's history of how it affected people in the 80's, while showing the characters struggling with problems that can be seen in the present-day, such as racism and poverty. What's important about the show is that it depicts people in the LGBTQ+ community in a humane and realistic way. Transgender characters in the show are important protagonists with depth and are played by real transgender actors. Even the supporting characters play important roles that aren't just for comic relief, which we've often seen being used as a joke in previous harmful media depictions that wouldn't be socially accepted today. For example, there's Blanca

Evangelista, the main protagonist who creates her own ballroom "house" to not only complete in the ballroom competitions, but to create a family of her own. She provides the guidance and support that she would've wanted when she was younger to her adopted "children." She even opens her own nail salon business after being fired from her previous job for attending a protest. We also have the eccentric Elektra Abundance, who is known for being reigning champion of New York's ballroom. She's known for being a narcissist and for making snarky remarks to other ballroom competitors that she sees as inferior. However, over the course of the show, we see her become a better person. She becomes more sympathetic and allows herself to be more vulnerable in front of her friends. Even if she sees herself as the queen, she is always willing to support her friends when they need it.

What's admirable about *Pose* is that they have increased the representation of transgender people by being responsible for 26 of the 29 transgender characters that are regularly on television, including 4 characters that are HIV or AIDS positive ("Where We on TV", 2020). The show has positively impacted its audience by giving people from the community someone they can relate to, something that makes them feel seen and heard. It has also helped fight the stigma on topics like HIV/AIDS. Even those who aren't part of the LGBTQ+ community are being educated and given an insightful look at what it's like for queer people behind the scenes.

Seeing transgender characters on television is great, but you know what's even better? Transgender characters being played by transgender actors. One of the problems in Hollywood is that many times when they're casting someone for an upcoming movie or show that has a transgender character, cisgender actors are usually the first to get considered for the role. It's not just transgender actors losing potential acting opportunities. This is happening with other sexualities and genders in the LGBTQ+ spectrum too. There's also the double standard where straight or cisgender actors are allowed to play queer roles, meanwhile, transgender actors are rarely given the chance to play a cisgender character. It's not that cisgender actors can't play queer roles, it's more about authenticity. No one truly knows what it's like to be transgender other than transgender people themselves. Giving cisgender actors these roles may exacerbate the harmful stigma that transgender people aren't real and that they're just people that are crossdressing or in drag. In 2018, Scarlett Johansson received backlash from the LGBTQ+ community when they announced that she would be playing the role of Dante "Tex" Gill, a trans man, in a movie called *"Rub & Tug"*. People felt that Gill would be misrepresented and were upset that another cisgender actress was taking an acting opportunity away from a potential trans actor. I believe they're right. It's sad to know that the first trans actress to play a transgender character on television (Laverne Cox) was just recently in 2017, and not earlier. Then there's MJ Rodriguez, who played the role of Blanca in *Pose*, who was the first trans actress to be nominated for an Emmy award in 2021. In *Variety Magazine*'s interview with Rodriguez, she described her nomination as something that "pushes the needle forward so much for now the door to be knocked down for so many people — whether they be male or trans female, gender nonconforming, LGBTQIA+" (Turchiano, 2021). If we continue down this route, barriers can be broken, and we can have better representation and storytelling from talented, queer actors.

Representation like this is so important because it reflects the way people outside the trans community see them and how transgender people see themselves. As of 2021, there are over 121 million American households that have a TV (Stoll, 2021), with the average person spending 3.1 hours a day watching television (Hubbard, 2021). We are constantly being exposed to media and it influences the way we see ourselves and the way we see others. TV can be a way for people to interconnect with different social groups like other ethnicities, race, culture, communities, or in this case, sexualities, and gender. Psychologically, what we see on tv can affect the way we interact with the world. In one form or another, people have a way of labeling themselves as part of a social group, whether it's something small like identifying as a fan of *Marvel* over *D.C Comics* or being a *Boston Red Sox* fan versus the *New York Yankees.* Or something bigger like being Christian versus Protestant, or American versus European. In psychology, everyone has two different categories of social groups. One is your in-group, the group that you socially identify with. The other is the out-group, the group that you don't associate yourself with. This often leads to intergroup bias, where people see their in-group as more favorable over the out-group. Sometimes it can go as far as creating rivalries, like how Democrats and Republicans see each other as political opponents. Both groups may start to display negative behaviors like discriminating against each other or thinking negative stereotypes. However, usually when the election is over, both parties can settle their differences and support the winning candidate, and in a way, become one group.

In this context, the two groups would be people who identify as part of the LGBTQ+ community and those who don't. With more exposure of this community on popular television, a bridge could be created to reduce the negative bias towards this community and be more open to their differences. Interpersonal contact can be a way to reduce prejudices and create positive attitudes. Even if the characters we see on television are fiction, there's some that have similar traits or lives to people in real life. It can significantly influence the way we perceive the people around us.

References

Adekaiyero, A. (2021, November 22). *Eddie Redmayne says 'it was a mistake' to play a trans character in 'The Danish Girl'*. Insider. Retrieved December 10, 2021, from https://www.insider.com/eddie-redmayne-says-mistake-play-trans-character-the-danish girl-2021-11.

Ayoub, Phillip M. "How the Media Has Helped Change Public Views about Lesbian and Gay People." *Scholars Strategy Network*, 24 May 2018, https://scholars.org/contribution/how media-has-helped-change-public-views-about-lesbian-and-gay-people.

Clifton, D. (2020, November 25). *Negative trans media depictions harm the community's mental health*. them. Retrieved December 10, 2021, from https://www.them.us/story/negative media-depictions-trans-people-harms-communitys-mental-health.

D'Addario, D. (2019, June 21). *Trans superstar Hunter Schafer on her moment of 'euphoria'*. Variety. Retrieved December 10, 2021, from https://variety.com/2019/tv/features/hunter schafer-hbo-euphoria-1203248330/.

Deerwater, Raina. "GLAAD's Where We Are on TV Report: Despite Tumultuous Year in Television, LGBTQ Representation Holds Steady." *GLAAD*, GLAAD, 14 Jan. 2021, https://www.glaad.org/blog/glaads-where-we-are-tv-report-despite-tumultuous-year television-lgbtq-representation-holds.

Ellis, Sarah Kate. "Procter & Gamble and GLAAD Study: Exposure to LGBTQ Representation in Media and Advertising Leads to Greater Acceptance of the LGBTQ Community." *GLAAD*, P&G, 27 May 2020, https://www.glaad.org/releases/procter-gamble-and-glaad study-exposure-lgbtq-representation-media-and-advertising-leads.

Flores, Andrew R. "Social Acceptance of LGBTI People in 175 Countries and Locations." *Williams Institute*, The Williams Institute, 8 Nov. 2021, https://williamsinstitute.law.ucla.edu/publications/global-acceptance-index-lgbt/.

Hubbard, K. (2021, July 22). *Americans spent more time watching television during COVID ...* U.S. News. Retrieved December 10, 2021, from https://www.usnews.com/news/best-states/articles/2021-07-22/americans-spent-more-time-watching-television-during-covid 19-than-working.

Hughto, J. M. W., Pletta, D., Gordon, L., Cahill, S., Mimiaga, M. J., & Reisner, S. L. (2021, January 12). *Negative transgender-related media messages are associated with adverse mental health outcomes in a Multistate Study of Transgender Adults*. LGBT health. Retrieved December 10, 2021, from https://www.ncbi.nlm.nih.gov/pmc/articles/PMC7826438/.

Kane, M. (2014, December 8). *GLAAD examines ten years of transgender images on television; more than half were negative or defamatory*. GLAAD. Retrieved December 10, 2021, from https://www.glaad.org/blog/glaad-examines-ten-years-transgender-images-television more-half-were-negative-or-defamatory.

Kelsey-Sugg, A. (2018, August 16). *Psychopaths, suicidal or comic relief: Problems with trans roles go beyond Scarlett Johansson*. ABC News. Retrieved December 10, 2021, from https://www.abc.net.au/news/2018-08-16/changing-media-representations-of-trans people/10114402.

Lil Nas X. "Lil Nas X - Thats What I Want (Official Video) - YouTube." *YouTube*, 17 Sept. 2021, https://www.youtube.com/watch?v=QDYDRA5JPLE.

Mocarski, R., King, R., Butler, S., Holt, N. R., Huit, T. Z., Hope, D. A., Meyer, H. M., & Woodruff, N. (2019, October 2). *The rise of transgender and gender diverse representation in the media: Impacts on the population*. Communication, culture & critique. Retrieved December 10, 2021, from https://www.ncbi.nlm.nih.gov/pmc/articles/PMC6824534/.

Official, Queen. "Queen - I Want To Break Free (Official Video)." *YouTube*, 1 Sept. 2008, Queen - I Want To Break Free (Official Video)

Oliver, D. (2020, November 27). *Hollywood's casting dilemma: Should straight, cisgender actors play LGBTQ characters?* USA Today. Retrieved December 10, 2021, from https://www.usatoday.com/story/entertainment/celebrities/2020/11/24/should-straight cisgender-actors-play-lgbtq-characters-in-hollywood/6327858002/.

Stoll, J. (2021, July 13). *TV households in U.S.* Statista. Retrieved December 10, 2021, from https://www.statista.com/statistics/243789/number-of-tv-households-in-the-us/.

Talusan, M. (2018, July 4). *Why Scarlett Johansson - or any CIS actor - should never play trans roles*. them. Retrieved December 10, 2021, from https://www.them.us/story/why-scarlett johansson-or-any-cis-actor-should-never-play-trans-roles.

Theodore. "Outgroup Bias (Definition + Examples)." *Practical Psychology*, Practical Psychology, 25 Oct. 2021, https://practicalpie.com/outgroup-bias-definition-examples/.

Turchiano, D. (2021, July 13). *MJ Rodriguez becomes first trans woman up for major acting Emmy*. Variety. Retrieved December 10, 2021, from https://variety.com/2021/tv/news/mj rodriguez-first-trans-woman-lead-acting-emmy-1235014189/.

Volsky, I. (2004, June 8). *Recalling Ronald Reagan's LGBT legacy ahead of the GOP presidential debate*. ThinkProgress. Retrieved December 14, 2021, from https://archive.thinkprogress.org/recalling-ronald-reagans-lgbt-legacy-ahead-of-the-gop presidential-debate-a687b80d679b/.

"Where We Are on TV Report: 2005 - 2006 Season." *GLAAD*, GLAAD, 11 Oct. 2018, https://www.glaad.org/publications/tvreport05.

Leaving Afghanistan: A Justified End

"On Aug. 1, 2009, while on one of those missions, Private Fitzgibbon stepped on a metal plate wired to a bomb buried in the sunbaked earth. The blue sky turned brown with dust. The explosion instantly killed Private Fitzgibbon, 19, of Knoxville, Tenn., and Cpl. Jonathan M. Walls, a 27-year-old father from Colorado Springs. An hour later, a third soldier who was helping secure the area, Pfc. Richard K. Jones, 21, of Roxboro, N.C., died from another hidden bomb. The two blasts wounded at least 10 other soldiers" ("Grim Milestone" 1). The tragic loss of American life in Afghanistan has been going on far too long, with the conflict now reaching its 20th anniversary. It is time to put a stop to the American fatalities. While the United States has invested countless dollars and far too many lives on the war in Afghanistan, these resources have seemingly been in vain as the Afghan people continually struggle to bolster a strong central government capable of providing freedom to their people independently. "On Tuesday [in 2010], the toll of American dead in Afghanistan passed 1,000, after a suicide bomb in Kabul killed at least five United States service members. Having taken nearly seven years to reach the first 500 dead, the war killed the second 500 in fewer than two. A resurgent Taliban active in almost every province, a weak central government incapable of protecting its people and a larger number of American troops in harm's way all contributed to the accelerating pace of death" ("Grim Milestone" 1). As American losses of all kinds continued after 2010 our course of action proved to be erroneous and our period of effectiveness in Afghanistan had concluded. These descriptions and statistics clearly portray that the United States was correct in withdrawing our troops from Afghanistan.

Opponents to this viewpoint have several arguments. First, they claim that withdrawing entirely was inappropriate and furthermore that doing so on a publicly announced schedule was needlessly harmful and gave the Taliban an immediate advantage. As Gearan mentions: "Since it became public Tuesday, Biden's decision has been criticized by many Republicans, who called it reckless or shortsighted. Pulling out U.S. troops, and announcing the specific timetable for doing so, will lead to victories by the Taliban and more terrorist acts, they warned" (1). Next, they argue that it is the responsibility of the United States to ensure the Afghan government does not collapse at any cost in order to deny the Taliban and its potential allies the ability to gain a strong foothold. As discussed in the article *Afghanistan War:* "At the very least, critics of withdrawal maintain, the United States must continue to provide Afghan forces enough intelligence and military support to prevent the Taliban from completely taking control of the country, a disaster that would have humanitarian, regional, and global repercussions. 'An American priority must be preventing the collapse of the Afghan government, lest the Taliban's partners, including al Qaeda and other jihadist terrorists, re-establish a base to plan, prepare and direct attacks against the U.S., its allies and others who don't conform to their perverted interpretation of Islam,' H.R. McMaster, a retired U.S. Army lieutenant general who served as a national security adviser to President Trump, and Bradley Bowman, senior director of the Hoover Institution, a think tank, wrote in the *Wall Street Journal* in July 2021" (1). Finally, they maintain that the Taliban, if in control, cannot be trusted to combat terrorist groups such as Al Qaeda in Afghanistan. Highlighted here in the article *Afghanistan War:* "The Taliban, opponents assert, cannot be trusted to keep Al Qaeda or other extremist groups out of Afghanistan. 'The idea that the U.S. can leave if the Taliban promise to combat rather than conspire with these groups is...wrongheaded,' retired U.S. Army general David Petraeus, who oversaw military operations in Afghanistan from July 2010 to July 2011, and Vance Serchuk, an adjunct senior fellow at the Center for a New American Security, a think tank, wrote in the *Wall Street Journal* in 2019" (1). The opposition claims that due to the reasons mentioned above we should continue to maintain a military presence in Afghanistan.

One reason the United States of America was correct in withdrawing our troops from Afghanistan is because their removal was a positive decision that will shift our country's attention to internal growth. As Gearan and others mention: "Biden did not declare a military victory, saying instead that a perpetual presence in the country would not serve U.S. interests. America must focus on a modern landscape of threats that is far different from that of nearly two decades ago, when the war began in response to the terrorist attacks of Sept. 11, 2001, Biden said. 'I'm now the fourth United States president to preside over American troop presence in Afghanistan. Two Republicans, two Democrats,' Biden said. 'I will not pass this responsibility on to a fifth.'... 'I've concluded that it's time to end America's longest war. It's time for American troops to come home,' he said... In his remarks, Biden said that each president who has dealt with the war has given a version of the same rationale for continuing to fight it. 'The main argument for staying longer is what each of my three predecessors have grappled with: No one wants to say that we should be in Afghanistan forever, but they insist now is not the right moment to leave,' he said" (1). Gearan and others are saying that over the last 20 years the international stage has changed drastically, and the wisest move is not for us to continue to remain in Afghanistan in a physical capacity. Touching on the idea that leaders of this country from both sides have had the opportunity to handle this complex issue in their own way and potentially find a permanent solution and so far, have not been able to, bringing our current leader to strongly state that our time to leave has arrived. Struye de Swielande continues: "It is unlikely that a Biden presidency would send large military contingents back to conflictual regions without any provocation or direct stake for the United States. Biden shares with Obama and Trump the idea of putting an end to endless wars with the withdrawal of soldiers from Syria, Iraq, and Afghanistan. Reducing the American military footprint in the world can prevent getting entangled in peripheral crises that would require boots on the ground at high cost and that would endanger the economic recovery" (Struye de Swielande, Tanguy, 6). This is relevant because it highlights the notion that these open-ended conflicts that began in the early 2000's are now coming to a close as America withdraws troops and reduces our military footprint in order to lower our 'entanglements' that can deal striking blows both in loss of life and financially. We are now beginning to look inward and put our economic success higher on the priority list. Lastly, Struye de Swielande states: "The all-out promotion of democracy and human rights since the 1990s has been characterized by numerous failures: the Rwanda genocide; wars in Somalia, Iraq, Afghanistan, and Libya; and the non-integration of Russia and China into the Western liberal order, to name but a few. Confidence in this order has collapsed, leaving the world in systemic chaos and ushering in a leadership vacuum and a crisis of legitimacy against the organizing principles of the order. In short, we are entering a period of rupture with the international order. Two possibilities can be delineated in such a context. The first possible path is to maintain the current course, continuing the head-in-the-sand policy that has characterized the United States and, even more so, Europe for several years, as these two poles of power have avoided acknowledging and adapting to new geopolitical realities and changes in the balance of power. The second possibility is to recognize this period of rupture as an opportunity, inspired by Schumpeter's (1962) process of creative destruction. This process consists in substituting an old dysfunctional model with a new, more efficient dynamic; it would make it possible to think and shape international relations from a balanced and realistic angle, as is increasingly acknowledged" (Struye de Swielande, Tanguy, 11-12). As discussed above, the long beloved American mission of promoting and delivering democracy around the world has left us over extended and shuffling resources out of the door that could be sorely used at home in important domestic matters as opposed to international conflict, Our 'head-in-the-sand' approach has seen countless resources and lives traded for very little permanent return. This withdrawal and dramatic variation from the norm of the last 20 years may be our new leadership attempting to embrace the idea mentioned of a 'period of rupture' becoming an opportunity to realign with the present times. Bringing new priorities and realistic expectations to international relations and turning our previous approach on its head entirely. Cumulatively these points all speak to the idea that putting an end to our physical presence in Afghanistan has the potential to launch America into a new era of international relations and allow our focus to shift onward to economic growth at home.

Another reason the United States was correct in withdrawing our troops from Afghanistan was that our military had accomplished their original mission, and it became clear that forcing democracy was not an obtainable objective. As Zucchino states: "In mid-April, President Joe Biden, declaring that the United States had long ago accomplished its mission of denying terrorists a safe haven in Afghanistan, announced that all U.S. troops would leave the country by Sept. 11. Biden said that after nearly 20 years of war, it was clear that the U.S. military could not transform Afghanistan into a modern, stable democracy. Responding in July to critics of the withdrawal, the president asked: 'Let me ask those who wanted us to stay: How many more? How many thousands more of America's daughters and sons are you willing to risk?'" (1). It is brought to light here that if American lives are going to be put on the line there must be a strong and very clear why. As President Biden said we cannot continue to write a blank check to Afghanistan when we have on many levels accomplished our original combat goal of not allowing the country to be a 'safe haven' for these terrorist groups in the area. It had become strikingly obvious that a strong democracy was not going to take root in the country despite our best efforts over nearly two decades, this goal was far beyond our reach. Bokat-Lindell and Spencer add: "Nearly two decades later, Peter Beinart argues in *The Times*, it is difficult for the United States to maintain its preferred image as a uniquely beneficent global actor. According to Brown University's Watson Institute for International and Public Affairs, post-Sept. 11 wars in which 'U.S. forces have been most significantly involved' have killed over 800,000 people, displaced 37 million and cost the United States some $6.4 trillion. (For reference, that is about $1.9 trillion more than the estimated cost of completely transitioning the U.S. power grid off fossil fuels)" (1). Here we see that while the United States is surely not to blame entirely for these statistics there is no doubt that our presence contributed, most likely significantly, to them. It is apparent that in our pursuit of imposing our democratic solution on Afghanistan we have continued to cause collateral damage while suffering our own losses, and in the meantime the cumulative result of our plans has not been as intended or satisfactory. Finally, Bokat-Lindell and Spencer mention: "Last week, Biden declined a request from Haiti's acting prime minister for military support following the assassination of that country's president, Jovenel Moïse. It was a decision that some commentators took as yet another sign of America's shrinking hegemony. 'The world's policeman is officially off duty,' Max Boot wrote in *The Washington Post*. 'After the fiascos of Iraq and Afghanistan, we have lost our appetite for democracy-building abroad. Biden doesn't use the slogan 'America First,' but he shares former President Donald Trump's aversion to nation-building and desire to end 'forever wars'" (1). Bokat-Lindell and Spencer make it clear here that President Biden is showing a great reluctance to step onto the international stage and intervene in foreign affairs. Entering the conflict in Haiti in an assisting role could quickly lead to attempting to bolster their young and struggling democracy that is experiencing turmoil following a violent assassination. It is becoming clear that there is no interest from America in this sort of activity after the failure to instate a strong democratic government in Afghanistan. All together it becomes clear that after achieving our initial goal in Afghanistan we remained in an attempt to deliver democracy that ultimately failed, and this failure has seemingly altered the course of American international relations for the foreseeable future as we attempt to understand our shortcomings and avoid similar situations.

A final reason the United States was correct in withdrawing our troops is because despite a massive investment on our part, enabling Afghans to defend their own country has proven ineffectual and no additional amount will change that outcome. As Zucchino discusses here: "Military and police units in Afghanistan have been hollowed out by desertions, low recruitment rates, poor morale, and the theft of pay and equipment by commanders. They have suffered high casualties, which U.S. commanders have said were not sustainable. Even though the United States has spent at least $4 billion a year on the Afghan military, a classified intelligence assessment presented to the Biden administration this spring said Afghanistan could fall largely under Taliban control within two to three years after the departure of international forces. The fall was much swifter than that, 'Afghanistan political leaders gave up and fled the country,' Biden said Monday, accusing the military of laying down arms after decades of U.S. training. 'If anything, the developments of the past week reinforce that ending U.S. military involvement in Afghanistan now was the right decision'" (qtd, in Zucchino 1). Zucchino is speaking on the fact that in a critical moment when a show of strength was required by Afghan military and political leadership, several high-ranking members chose to desert their country and leave those that remained disoriented and at a great disadvantage to the Taliban forces who were able to capitalize on this vulnerability. While it was expected that a few years down the line there would be a serious power struggle that may lead to the country being under Taliban control, no one expected the mass exodus of leadership that occurred. This speaks highly to the idea that despite the constant efforts from American forces to build a strong Afghan military force there is clearly an intangible, and possibly several, missing pieces that we cannot simply train into the population, meaning any extended presence would be continuing to mindlessly dedicate time, effort, and resources in a futile attempt to establish a democracy and a functioning, effective military in a land with no precedent for it. O'Donnell adds: "Afghan forces are struggling to man the front lines against a resurgent Taliban, in part because of untold numbers of 'ghost' troops who are paid salaries but only exist on paper. The nationwide problem has been particularly severe in the southern Helmand province, where the Taliban have seized vast tracts of territory in the 12 months since the U.S. and NATO formally ended their combat mission and switched to training and support. 'At checkpoints where 20 soldiers should be present, there are only eight or 10,' said Karim Atal, head of Helmand's provincial council. 'It's because some people are getting paid a salary but not doing the job because they are related to someone important, like a local warlord.' In some cases, the "ghost" designation is more literal—dead soldiers and police remain on the books, with senior police or army officials pocketing their salaries without replacing them, Atal said" (qtd. in O'Donnell 1). This quote addresses the rampant corruption present at all levels in the Afghan military. Without the support of American forces to fill the gaps and hide these inconsistencies, truly concerning behaviors are being brought to the world's attention. From troops themselves with strong family ties not being required to report, all the way to high-ranking members not reporting casualties and simply taking the pay of their deceased subordinates, the Afghan military is severely handicapping themselves in the fight against the Taliban and revealing their true shades. Those that are present and willing to sacrifice life and limb are being betrayed by those who are supposed to be next to them on the front lines and allowing the enemy to take massive swathes of territory at the same time. Finally, Zucchino points out: "In many cases, they surrendered without a fight, sometimes following the intercession of village elders sent by the Taliban. Thousands of Afghans, frightened of reprisal killings, tried on Monday to flee the country, seeking refuge at Kabul's international airport, which was held by foreign military forces trying to assist with evacuations. The Afghan government's collapse, after the United States spent billions to support it and Afghan security forces, was a violent coda to the U.S. military mission in America's longest war. That combat mission dogged four presidents, who reckoned with American casualties, a ruthless enemy and an often-confounding Afghan partner" (1). The sentiment here is that the overall morale of the people is suffering from a lack of true desire to resist the Taliban, such as the village elders who have seemingly sided with the Taliban forces and served as message bearers encouraging a peaceful surrender or those that are overrun with fear of excessive violence from the Taliban and will not step up to fight. With American forces out of the country the Afghan military has seemingly fallen victim to a lack of conviction and possibly through a lack of understanding of the complex social dynamics present throughout the country or other factors we were not able to prepare them to stand independently. However, this has also demonstrated that if we could not achieve this in 20 years it is doubtful that we would ever have been able to. Through these points it is apparent that although we have committed an overwhelming amount of resources, time, and human lives in order to try and cultivate a government and military capable of resisting the Taliban and defending their own country, the components that are lacking cannot simply be acquired through the various methods that we have employed over the last 20 years, making the present as good a time as there ever will be to withdraw our troops.

As discussed in these arguments, the United States was correct in withdrawing its military from Afghanistan. While the opposition claims that the information on the withdrawal plan was too public, that we needed to maintain a presence to ensure the Afghan government did not fall, and that we should not have trusted the Taliban to not allow terrorist groups to take haven in the country, these arguments are not strong enough to rationalize our physical presence in Afghanistan. First, we were correct in withdrawing because the removal of our forces will allow us to dedicate more resources and attention domestically instead of sending them overseas to serve a 20-year war that could have been-continued for another 20 years easily. Furthermore, we were justified because we had accomplished our original mission of denying terrorist organizations easily accessible safe havens in Afghanistan, while our secondary goal of establishing a strong democracy was revealed to be no longer feasible. Finally, the decision was proper because after endless investments, the Afghan people still appear to be ultimately unwilling to sustain their own freedom and have created several obstacles that any continuing military support from America would only delay and never fully resolve in any permanent capacity. As expressed throughout these arguments, while the situation in Afghanistan is far from resolved, our role and contributions have gone far enough, and often without comparable return from the Afghan people, to justify our withdrawal. Our desired plan for the country, a strong central democracy, would never become viable with the citizens of the country. Now the future lies in the hands of the remaining Afghan leaders, and we can only hope that they become revitalized and do not entirely squander the past 20 years of resources and training, and instead combat the Taliban and assemble some form of government that every man, woman, and child can feel protected, represented, and proud to be united underneath.

Works Cited

Bokat-Lindell, Spencer. "Is the United States Done Being the World's Cop?" *New York Times*, 20 Jul. 2021. https://ccsu.idm.oclc.org/login?url=https://www.proquest.com/blogs-podcasts-websites/is-united-states-done-being-world-s-cop/docview/2553351600/se-2?accountid=9970.

Gearan, Anne et al. "Biden Tells Americans 'We Cannot Continue the Cycle' in Afghanistan as He Announces Troop Withdrawal" *The Washington Post,* 14 Apr. 2021. https://ccsu.idm.oclc.org/login?url=https://www.proquest.com/blogs-podcasts-websites/biden-tells-americans-we-cannot-continue-cycle/docview/2512593993/se-2?accountid=9970.

Struye de Swielande, Tanguy. "The Biden Administration: An Opportunity to Affirm a Flexible and Adaptive American World Leadership." World Affairs, vol. 184, no. 2, Summer 2021, pp. 130–150.

Zucchino, David. "Twenty Years, Four Presidents and a Mission that Went Awry." *New York Times*, 16 Aug. 2021. https://ccsu.idm.oclc.org/login?url=http://www.proquest.com/newspapers/twenty-years-four-presidents-mission-that-went/docview/2561599834/se-2?accountid=9970.

"Afghanistan War: Was the United States Right to Have Withdrawn from Afghanistan" *Issues & Controversies*, Infobase, 31 Aug. 2021, icof.infobase.com/articles/QXJ0aWNsZVRleHQ6MTYYlNDc=. Accessed 7 Dec. 2021.

"Grim Milestone: 1,000 Americans Dead." *New York Times*, 18 May. 2010. https://ccsu.idm.oclc.org/login?url=https://www.proquest.com/blogs-podcasts-websites/grim-milestone-1-000-americans-dead/docview/2218673592/se-2?accountid=9970.

O'Donnell, Lynne, and Mirwais Khan. "Afghan Army's 'Ghost Soldiers'; Troops are on the Books, but Exist Only on Paper. Taliban has Taken Advantage." *Los Angeles Times*, 17 Jan. 2016. ProQuest, https://ccsu.idm.oclc.org/login?url=https://www.proquest.com/newspapers/afghan-armys-ghost-soldiers-troops-are-on-books/docview/1757498747/se-2?accountid=9970.

The United States was Wrong to Withdraw from Afghanistan

"Al-Qaeda's strength and ability to strike the West has significantly diminished over the past decade, but its leader Ayman al-Zawahiri is believed to still be based in Afghanistan along with a number of other senior figures in the group. The Afghan intelligence services announced on Saturday they had killed Husam Abd al-Rauf, a high-ranking Egyptian al-Qaeda member, in an operation in Ghazni province. Mr. Fitton-Brown told the BBC that despite its lower profile, al-Qaeda remained `resilient' and 'dangerous' (qtd. In "Al-Qaeda Still 'Heavily Embedded' within Taliban in Afghanistan, UN Official Warns Page 1). The United States first entered Afghanistan in 2001 with the purpose of tracking down and kill those responsible for 9/11. This turned out to be Al-Qaeda with Osama bin Laden at the forefront. Although he has been eliminated, the group itself has not. They are still active and in Afghanistan. They have been marginalized with American presence. However, what will happen now when the Taliban take over? Will they work with the existing government, or will they rule with brute force as they did in the past? Furthermore, will they allow their extremist allies to regain power in the area? As we now know, our worst fears are now manifesting, the Taliban have shown to continue to have ties to al-Qaeda. With their complete takeover of the Afghanistan government and the continual rule with an iron and brutal fist, they are permitting their extremist allies to establish havens to build their strength and plan attacks in the west. As states in "By the Numbers": "Approximate number of Afghan civilians killed in Afghanistan War 50,000" (1). While tens of thousands of Afghanis were collateral damage during the U.S. presence in Afghanistan, many more will likely suffer under the merciless rule of the Taliban. Freedom and democracy; which the U.S. had worked to establish, have come to an abrupt end, replaced with brutal punishment for minor infractions of the Taliban's interpretation of Sharia law. Together, these arguments support the conclusion that the United States should not have withdrawn its troops from Afghanistan for the safety of the Afghanistan and American people the United States should not have withdrawn from Afghanistan.

The first reason as to why the United States should have not withdrawn its military from Afghanistan is to protect the people of Afghanistan from the Taliban's unethical rule. In "Afghanistan War Was the United States Right to Have Withdrawn from Afghanistan?" it states: "The Taliban resurgence was particularly strong in Helmand, a southern province where corruption and abuse of power among administrators appointed by Karzai had fueled popular discontent. In Helmand and other provinces, the Taliban infiltrated villages, secured the loyalty of local elders, and assassinated officials or villagers with suspected allegiances to the Afghan state or ISAF" (1). This shows the basic civil liberties that are being broken Everday under Taliban rule. The people are ruled with an iron fist and any that speak out are killed on the spot. This is no way for humans to live and should not be allowed to occur. A withdrawal only exemplifies these examples and every day since America left, we continue to have blood on our hands. The article also adds: "A stark rise in insurgent attacks in 2006 raised doubts that Karzai's government and international forces were capable of protecting civilians from a seemingly resurgent Taliban. That year, the number of suicide bombings and the use of improvised explosive devices (IEDs)—which blow up by remote control or upon being stepped on or driven over—skyrocketed in comparison to previous years. To carry out suicide bombings, the Taliban often recruited poor and mentally handicapped young men, as well as fighters seeking revenge for family members who had died in coalition bombings or raids. Recruits studied in Pakistani madrassas where they learned they would be rewarded in the afterlife for carrying out such attacks" (1). This quote is important because it shows the disregard of life the Taliban have. They would recruit people who are at their absolute lowest and promise them a good ending of they wear an IED and blow-up innocent civilians. They are cruel, oppressive leaders and America lets them gain control of a country with millions of innocent people. Finally, in "Al-Qaeda Still 'Heavily Embedded' within Taliban in Afghanistan, UN Official Warns" it states: "It is feared the Afghan peace process is in any case losing its momentum. Despite the beginning of long delayed negotiations between the Taliban and an Afghan government-led delegation last month in Qatar, violence has continued and even intensified in recent weeks. The negotiations have stalled amid attempts to resolve preliminary issues, with major issues such as a ceasefire or power-sharing arrangement yet to be discussed. There are fears that if US troops are withdrawn next year, before an agreement has been reached, the violence could intensify and the Taliban push for a military victory" (Secunder 4). This quote shows to the unwillingness of the Taliban to work towards a resolution. They are not people who can be persuaded or are ready to compromise. They want to rule the way they want, which has been proven to be an oppressive regime. The American withdrawal left a country without the means or money to defend itself from an enemy that wants nothing more than to see the people be oppressed. As these points indicate, a total withdrawal from Afghanistan is a horrible idea that will lead to a major human rights crisis which should not occur. It is America's duty to protect freedom for all and that is the exact opposite of what happened during the withdrawal. We made the conscious decision to let the Afghanistan people be oppressed.

Another reason as to why the United States should not have pulled out of Afghanistan is because a retreat would damage our reputation on the world stage. According to Lisa Curtis, the director of the indo-pacific security program states in an interview with Vox: "'The first option would be what you presented as pulling out all US troops. That would risk a civil war, the reemergence of a terrorist safe haven, and a tremendous loss of US credibility built with our allies'" (qtd. In Ward 3). This quote from Curtis explains how leaving Afghanistan has made us appear weak and disloyal. It will reduce the esteem and respect with which the United States has been regarded by many because other people around the world who rely on our aide will examine the situation that unfolded in Afghanistan and will wonder if we would treat them the same way we treated the Afghani's if we agreed to supply military assistance. This could lead to not as many people wanting to help because they will be worried that we will abandon them as we did the Afghani's. This could mean that the US is viewed more negatively throughout the world. Curtis also adds: "'Let's not forget that the US provides moral support, too. Having the US there is a source of reassurance for the Afghans. The minute the US says, "we're going to zero troops," you're going to see a lot of Afghans flee the country, You're probably going to see a refugee crisis, which the Europeans are really worried about. There are a lot of impacts that happen when the US takes that ultimate step of going to zero'" (qtd. In Ward 3). Curtis once again identifies the myriad negative consequences that could, and have, resulted from our withdrawal from Afghanistan. Our perceived betrayal of Afghanistan will mean a deluge of refugees descending on our allies in Europe. Given the large numbers who have and will seek to flee, a refugee crisis may well occur and add on to the immigration crisis currently occurring in Europe, This will not enhance our relations with our allies in Europe and elsewhere. Finally, Secunder, states in "Al-Qaeda still 'Heavily Embedded' within Taliban in Afghnaistan, UN official warns." that: "One diplomat closely observing the process told the BBC the US withdrawal plans were no longer 'condition based' but 'agenda based', suggesting President Trump's overriding priority is to end America's longest-ever war. At times President Trump has appeared out of step with military advisers, recently criticizing defense officials who, he said, 'want to do nothing but fight wars" (4). This quote demonstrates that Trump's motivations may have had nothing to do with military objectives, the welfare of the Afghans, or our national security. Rather the priority for Trump was to secure his re-election. A withdrawal negotiated on this basis would be morally and ethically reprehensible and would damage our relations with our allies worldwide, never mind causing great harm to the people of Afghanistan. All this information points towards that a total withdrawal from Afghanistan would negatively impact our global reputation and could harm our relations with present and future allies.

A final reason as to why the United States should have maintained a military presence in Afghanistan is to stop the creation of the most dangerous safe haven for extremists the world has ever seen. In "Al-Qaeda Still 'Heavily Embedded' within Taliban in Afghanistan, UN Official Warns" it states: "But Edmund Fitton-Brown, coordinator of the UN's Islamic State, Al-Qaeda and Taliban Monitoring Team, has told the BBC that the Taliban promised al-Qaeda in the run-up to the US agreement that the two groups would remain allies" (4). This is particularly important because it shows that even when the Taliban had made the deal with America on the withdrawal that they were still allied to the group responsible for 9/11. The group has already committed the worst terrorist attack in American history and now they will have free reign to regain power in the lawless Afghanistan. In "Afghanistan War Was the United States Right to Have Withdrawn from Afghanistan?" it states: "And, as we know, in 2011, America hastily and mistakenly withdrew from Iraq. As a result, our hard-won gains slipped back into the hands of terrorist enemies. Our soldiers watched as cities they had fought for, and bled to liberate, and won, were occupied by a terrorist group called ISIS. The vacuum we created by leaving too soon gave safe haven for ISIS to spread, to grow, recruit, and launch attacks. We cannot repeat in Afghanistan the mistake our leaders made in Iraq" (1). This shows that we have prior knowledge of what a hastily withdrawal could cause. The Taliban in control could lead to other extremists' groups rising to power. They could be bigger and stronger than others we have delt with in the past. This quick withdrawal could also lead the U.S. to be forced to re-enter Afghanistan to destroy a new threat. This could lead to thousands of more American deaths and the start of a new war. Finally in Curtis's Interview with Vox she says: "But remember also that if the Taliban came back to power, you'll see terrorists from all over the world — not just al Qaeda—you'll see a convergence of extremists and terrorists back in Afghanistan. It's likely to be a worse terrorist safe haven than it was before 9/11" (qtd. In Ward 3). This quote shows the frightening realization that a withdrawal could cause lots of innocent lives to be lost. Afghanistan would become a hideout for the worst groups to ever walk this earth and there would be no one there to keep them in place.

Without American forces in Afghanistan the extremists can become enormously powerful and as states even more powerful than before the 9/11 attacks which means that thousands of innocent lives are now in danger Everday. This evidence points towards that due to the American withdrawal from Afghanistan It is now expected that extremists from all around the world will now have a location to be grow and gain power which they will then use to attack the west and all its people.

There are some arguments used by the people who think the United States were right to pull out of Afghanistan. First, they argue that The United States has spent so much tax dollars in Afghanistan already and has gotten us nowhere. As stated in "Afghanistan War": "The Costs of War, a team of scholars and legal experts, estimates that the United States has spent more than $2 trillion on military operations, aid and reconstruction efforts, and care for veterans of the conflict" (1). Second, they maintain the number of Americans killed or injured is already too high. According to "By the Numbers", approximately 2500 men and women lost their lives in Afghanistan, and thousands more were wounded (2). The Third and final argument is that we have been in Afghanistan for two decades and early on accomplished our original goal. Since then, we have invested tremendous resources in attempting to dislodge and subdue the Taliban, Without success. Our effort there had simply become a losing battle. As President Biden stated: "My fellow Americans, the war in Afghanistan is now over. I'm the fourth President who has faced the issue of whether and when to end this war. When I was running for President, I made a commitment to the American people that I would end this war. And today, I've honored that commitment. It was time to be honest with the American people again. We no longer had a clear purpose in an open-ended mission in Afghanistan. After 20 years of war in Afghanistan, I refused to send another generation of America's sons and daughters to fight a war that should have ended long ago. After more than $2 trillion spent in Afghanistan—a cost that researchers at Brown University estimated would be over $300 million a day for 20 years in Afghanistan—for two decades—yes, the American people should hear this: $300 million a day for two decades.... We've been a nation too long at war. If you're 20 years old today, you have never known an America at peace" (US gov 5). For these reasons there are many people who believe it was right to withdraw from Afghanistan.

All these reasons led to one conclusion the United States was wrong to withdraw its military from Afghanistan. While the opposition will argue that we have already invested so much time and money as well as lost so many American and Afghani lives in this 20 yearlong war that a withdraw must occur, they are wrong. Because yes, a lot of money and time was spent as well as a lot of lives lost but those were invested into a prize which we cannot see which is safety. Without those continued sacrifices the United States and its allies could be in danger. First, it was wrong to pull out of Afghanistan because it is our duty as Americans to help out those in need. We should act to maintain basic human rights for all so that all humans can live their best lives. We should not let the Taliban infringe upon the Afghanistan people. In Addition, A complete withdrawal from Afghanistan will make us look bad in the eyes of the world. This could lead to some serious complications down the road especially with our allies when they are unsure if they can trust that we will be by their side when they need us the most or we will just abandon them like we did to the Afghanistan people. Finally, the United States should not have pulled out because without our presence there and the Taliban in control Afghanistan will become a safe haven for extremist groups like Al-Qaeda which could spell disaster for the free world. These reasons show that despite, the money, time, and lives lost there is still a need for the United States to be in Afghanistan. The Afghanistan government is not ready to handle the Taliban yet and they might not be for many years, but that time would be worth the wait because this shouldn't be about some political points to cash in latter. This is about people's lives and the safety of innocent civilians and money, and time should not be more important than making sure people have the basic right to live.

Works Cited

"Afghanistan War." *Issues and Controversies,* Infobase, 31 Aug. 2021, icof.infobase.com/articles/QXJ0aWNsZVR1eHQ6MTY1NDc=. Accessed 1 Nov. 2021.

"By the Numbers: Afghanistan War." *Issues and Controversies,* Infobase, 30 Aug. 2021, icof.infobase.com/articles/QXJ0aWNsZVR1eHQ6MTcxMDQ=. Accessed 21 Nov. 2021.

Kermani, Secunder. "Al-Qaeda Still 'Heavily Embedded' within Taliban in Afghanistan, UN Official Warns," *BBC News,* BBC, 29 Oct. 2020, https://www.bbc.com/news/world-asia-547114525.

United States, White House. *Remarks by President Biden on the End of the War in Afghanistan.* 31 Aug. 2021, https://www.whitehouse.gov/briefing-room/speeches-remarks/2021/08/31/remarks-by_president-biden-on-the-end-of-the-war-in-afghanistan/.

Ward, Alex. "The Best Case against Withdrawing All US Troops from Afghanistan." *Vox,* Vox, 17 Mar. 2021, https://www.vox.com/22327124/afghanistan-troop-withdrawal-biden-lisa-curtis-stay.

The Academic Struggles of Living with Anxiety: A Study of the Effect of Clinical Anxiety on High School Teenagers

Abstract

This report examines and answers the following research question: How does medically diagnosed anxiety affect the academic progress of American high school students? Investigation of this topic led to the thesis that American high school students with anxiety can experience patterns of impulsive and/or over-thinking, a lack of social skills, and an absence of appropriate treatment, which can all negatively-affect their academic progress. 2.2% of American adolescents aged 13-18 are diagnosed with Generalized Anxiety Disorder and 9.1% are diagnosed with Social Anxiety Disorder. This statistic exhibits the fact that more adolescents have anxiety than people think, so it is important to bring attention to the problems that those in an anxious state-of-mind have to deal with.

I. Purpose

This research question is important to those with medically diagnosed anxiety because people without anxiety do not completely understand what they go through. A common example of misunderstanding the hardships that come with anxiety is someone saying, "Just try not to think about it!" One may think that it is easy to deal with this condition, but there are many factors that go into the cause of someone's anxiety and many obstacles that make it harder to become less anxious. This research study will allow those who do not have medically diagnosed anxiety to learn about the day-to-day challenges, symptoms, and/or negative effects that anxious high-schoolers face when in an academic setting, and, hopefully, will raise awareness about living with this condition and how to supplement and care for those who have it.

II. Methods

The most useful article pertaining to this research was, "The Relationship between Negative Urgency and Generalized Anxiety Disorder Symptoms: the Role of Intolerance of Negative Emotions and Intolerance of Uncertainty" by Elizabeth Pawluk and Naomi Koerner. This article showed to be most useful due to the authors covering two different sides of how a person with anxiety thinks and acts. While it is fairly known that people with anxiety tend to over-think situations, the authors also mention how they can think and act impulsively because they cannot deal with their own emotions, nor uncertainty. This interesting viewpoint helps bring awareness to the troubles that high school students with medically diagnose anxiety may face because it explains their thought-process and the reasons for their actions in certain situations. In other words, the article helps those without anxiety understand what it is like to live with that disorder.

III. Findings

While high school is already known, by most, to be one of the hardest phases of life, it is even more difficult to tolerate in concurrence with a medically diagnosed anxiety disorder. Although it may go unnoticed by teachers and fellow classmates, those with anxiety are battling different circumstances every day. These circumstances, in turn, can set off many reactions that range from avoidance, to panic, to completely shutting oneself down. American high school students with anxiety can experience patterns of impulsive and/or over-thinking, a lack of social skills, and an absence of appropriate treatment, which can all negatively affect their academic progress.

There are several different forms of medically diagnosed anxiety; however, two of the most common forms are Generalized Anxiety Disorder (GAD) and Social Anxiety Disorder (SAD). According to the American Psychiatric Association, GAD is characterized as, "… persistent and excessive worry that interferes with daily activities," whereas SAD is characterized as, "… anxiety and discomfort about being embarrassed, humiliated, rejected or looked down on in social situations." To officially be diagnosed with one of these disorders, one should first have a discussion with their doctor; a doctor can help their patients work through troubling matters and provide them with the appropriate resources, such as a qualified therapist, psychologist, or even a mental-health group. Once personal situations are spoken about with a doctor, tests such as assessment measures can be carried out to diagnose the disorder, such as a severity test where questions regarding thought, feelings, and behaviors are answered by the patient or must be filled out by a clinician ("What are Anxiety Disorders?").

Anxiety is usually associated with the symptom of over-thinking situations, meaning easy tasks in school can become much harder than they are supposed to be. It is extremely difficult for someone in a state of caution to effectively evaluate benefits and drawbacks and form a valid decision. In turn, ideas can be easily misinterpreted and the wrong actions can be taken. This problem can prevent someone from growing academically as they focus too much on irrelevant details and struggle to grasp main concepts. Pawluk and Koerner of Ryerson University in Canada state, "GAD symptoms display a need to gather a large amount of information before making a decision, even when the decision is relatively inconsequential," (qtd. in Tallis et al.). With this kind of mindset, a high school student with GAD can have difficulties in classes where they must provide their own opinion or give reasons for an answer. The format of gathering information can cause them to go too far in depth and not be able to make a decision, but rather confuse themselves about the question being asked and take it too literally. Multiple choice questions can also become a nuisance because of how closely-related some answers may be. By over-thinking, students can diminish their understanding of topics and focus too little on what is really important.

Although people with GAD tend to over-think situations and make decisions too slowly, intolerance of uncertainty and of one's own negative emotions can also cause them to have impulsive thinking, leading to a reduction in positive academic performance. Since negative emotions can be unwanted but occur uncontrollably, a high school student may find it easier to completely shut down or avoid the problem as much as possible. Additionally, a high level of uncertainty can cause them to act impulsively than to deal with the problem at hand. Pawluk and Koerner say that as, "… their capacity for rational reasoning is diminished, their attention is directed to immediate rather than long-term consequences, and they prioritize rapid modification of their intense discomfort, even when they know these actions are likely to be counter-productive in the longer run" (611). For example, lots of high school students regularly procrastinate because they're too lazy to work on an assignment. However, a high school student with GAD would procrastinate because they cannot tolerate their emotions of worry that the assignment is too hard, will take too long, or the possibility of receiving a low grade on it. Even though the decision to procrastinate will negatively affect the quality of their assignment in the long-run, they are doing what is best for themselves in the short-run—eliminating their excessive worry.

Along with over-thinking, a lack of social skills can negatively affect a high school student's ability to participate in class. It is normal to have a small amount of fear of being embarrassed, but when a student has SAD, they will have excessive fear and try to avoid situations they deem embarrassing as much as possible. A study conducted by Mehtalia and Vankar in India showed that out of a group of 421 high school students, 54 were diagnosed with SAD (222). Among these 54 students, it was most commonly reported that, "Being criticized scares [them] a lot… [They are] afraid of doing things when people might be watching… Being embarrassed or looking stupid are among [their] worst fears… [They] would do anything to avoid being criticized" (Mehtalia and Vankar 223). With this type of mentality, a high school student with SAD would surely have trouble with school performance. For instance, avoiding certain situations such as class presentations or discussions would cause a decrease in one's participation grade. Choosing to not participate, such as by asking questions, would also diminish a student's understanding of class concepts because they are, now, not able to fully comprehend what is being taught, which means they will also not be able to apply that lesson to future assignments.

Even worse, the act of avoiding social situations can form a cycle that continuously damages a high school student's academic abilities. This cycle begins when the student first avoids the situations they are afraid of. In turn, their grades and knowledge are negatively-affected, which could cause them to avoid these situations even more because they do not have the experience to prepare themselves for those circumstances. Luigi Mazzone, member of the Department of Child Neurology and Psychiatry in Italy, insists that, "While poor school performance can result from excessive anxiety, it can also be itself the cause of anxiety, low self-esteem, and other affective symptoms, thus creating a self-maintaining cycle" (2). This cycle explains how a student may become trapped even further in their anxiety as it is fed exactly by what they are avoiding. Because of the continuous cycle, students will never be prepared for social interactions in school, such as working in groups, and will face more and more side-effects the longer the cycle runs for.

The greatest thing that can affect a high school student's academic achievements is not receiving the proper or appropriate amount of treatment for their anxiety. It is important for everyone, whether they have medically diagnosed anxiety or not, to keep in mind that anxiety is a real disorder that does negatively impact those who have it. Without this understanding, it can be extremely difficult for a student with anxiety to acquire the correct form of treatment as the extent of their disorder is either not believed by others, or they have a hard time, in general, finding the most effective treatment for themselves. Research supports the idea that, "… compared to anxious youth who did not receive treatment, youth who received cognitive behavioral therapy showed improvements in academic motivation (qtd. in Keough et al.), standardizes test scores (qtd. in Keough et al.), GPA (qtd. in Weems et al.), and teacher and parent ratings of general academic functioning" (Nail et al. 329). It is vital for those with medically diagnosed anxiety to undergo treatment as it can not only improve their personal well-being, but also improve their academic success and prevent them from falling behind in school. Receiving treatment can further be translated into having better academic success in college as well; an increase in academic motivation will allow the students to perform well in their classes by not only scoring higher on exams and receiving higher grades, but also increasing their knowledge and understanding of what they learn. Thus, college courses related to these high school topics will become easier for students who struggle with anxiety.

Understanding the challenges of living with medically diagnosed anxiety is important in America's society as 2.2% of adolescents aged 13-18 are diagnosed with GAD, and 9.1% of adolescents are diagnosed with SAD ("Social Anxiety Disorder"). Students are faced with struggles every day as they anticipate the worst of their fears and are forced to protect themselves in a state of caution. Due to this cautious response, a student's academic progress is negatively-effected as their anxiety lessons their ability to work in a school environment.

IV. Discussion

As someone who struggles with anxiety, I believe that it is vital to understand what those with medically diagnosed anxiety go through on a daily basis in school. This report has proved that anxiety is not easy to control as it can be detrimental to a high school student's academic progress. Anxiety could potentially cause a student to drop out of high school, which further affects their future. Without a high school diploma, a student will not be able to attend college and may find it hard to apply for certain jobs in the long-run. Overall, I demonstrate empathy for those with medically diagnosed anxiety because I feel as though I can relate to them and have experienced the same troubles.

What matters most is providing the right help for those with anxiety. One of the most common ways people deal with anxiety is by taking a medication. Although the medication will not cure the disorder, it can lessen the symptoms and make one's life less troublesome. Common medications that can be taken are anti-anxiety medications and antidepressants. Since these medications are prescribed, one must consult a doctor beforehand. Consulting with a doctor may also allow the patient to receive help and guidance with choosing the right medication (APA).

Although medications will not treat anxiety, a common way that will is psychotherapy. One example of psychotherapy is Cognitive Behavioral Therapy (CBT). With this routine, a psychologist helps to identify one's negative thinking and behavior patterns that could be causing harm and worsening their anxiety. The psychologist, in turn, will help their patient develop skills and a different outlook to prevent their anxiety and change the way they respond to certain situations (APA).

Word Count: 2,146

Works Cited

Asgari, Masoumeh, et al. "Prevalence of Social Phobia Disorder in High School Students in Abhar City, Iran." *Journal of Fundamentals of Mental Health*, vol. 18, no. 1, Jan. 2016, pp. 42–47. *Academic Search Premier*, search.ebscohost.com/login.aspx?direct=true&db =aph&AN=117066905&site=ehost-live&scope=site.

Fisher, Paige H., et al. "Skills for Social and Academic Success: A School-Based Intervention for Social Anxiety Disorder in Adolescents." *Clinical Child & Family Psychology Review*, vol. 7, no. 4, Dec. 2004, pp. 241–249. *Academic Search Premier*, doi:10.1007/ s10567-004-6088-7.

Mehtalia, Khyati, and G. K. Vankar. "Social Anxiety in Adolescents." *Indian Journal of Psychiatry*, vol. 46, no. 3, July 2004, pp. 221–227. *PubMed*, search.ebscohost.com/login. aspx?direct=true&db=cmedm&AN=21224903&site=ehost-live&scope=site.

Pawluk, Elizabeth J., and Naomi Koerner. "The Relationship between Negative Urgency and Generalized Anxiety Disorder Symptoms: The Role of Intolerance of Negative Emotions and Intolerance of Uncertainty." *Anxiety, Stress & Coping*, vol. 29, no. 6, Nov. 2016, pp. 606–615. *Academic Search Premier*, doi:10.1080/10615806.2015.1134786.

Mazzone, Luigi, et al. "The Role of Anxiety Symptoms in School Performance in a Community Sample of Children and Adolescents." *BMC Public Health*, vol. 7, no. 1, 5 Dec. 2007, pp. 1–6. *PubMed*, doi:10.1186/1471-2458-7-347.

Nail, Jennifer, et al. "Academic Impairment and Impact of Treatments Among Youth with Anxiety Disorders." *Child & Youth Care Forum*, vol. 44, no. 3, June 2015, pp. 327–342. *Academic Search Premier*, doi:10.1007/s10566-014-9290-x.

"What Are Anxiety Disorders?" *American Psychiatric Association*, www.psychiatry.org/ patients-families/anxiety-disorders/what-are-anxiety-disorders.

"Generalized Anxiety Disorder." *National Institute of Mental Health*, U.S. Department of Health and Human Services, https://www.nimh.nih.gov/health/statistics/generalized-anxiety-disorder.shtml.

"Social Anxiety Disorder." *National Institute of Mental Health*, U.S. Department of Health and Human Services, https://www.nimh.nih.gov/health/statistics/social-anxiety-disorder.shtml.

INDEX